3D Articulation
Using OpenGL
moving parts & hair

Book 3 in the 3D Rendering Series

by D. James Benton

Preface

This is a third course on three-dimensional rendering of models, building on my previous books, *3D Rendering in Windows* and *3D Models in Motion*. In this text we will cover spatial manipulation of objects in order to create the appearance of specific articulation. We also cover finer details, including hair or fur. The Windows® operating system and OpenGL® rendering engine will be our platform, but the same principles apply equally well to other environments. We assume the reader is familiar with C and programming for the Windows® operating system and will not dwell on those details. Many references are available on these foundational subjects, including my book, *Version Independent Programming*. As in that text, we require that all code function properly on any version and configuration of Windows®. All of the software and associated files described herein is available free online.

All of the examples contained in this book,
(as well as a lot of free programs) are available at...
https://www.dudleybenton.altervista.org/software/index.html

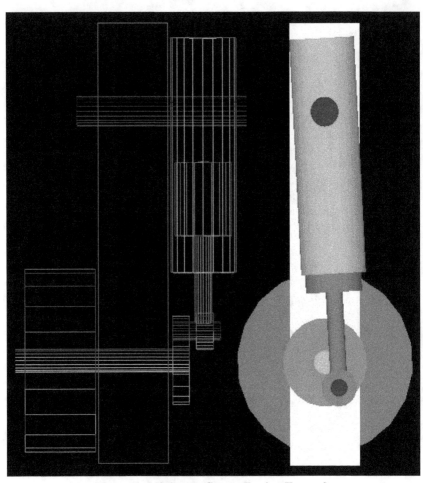

Figure 1. Miniature Steam Engine Example
Discussed in Chapter 1
based on the work of Troy Robinette

Table of Contents

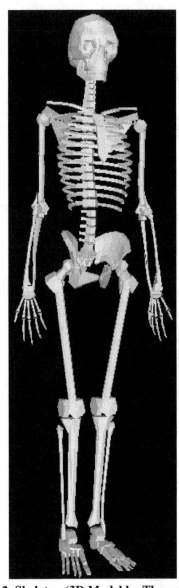

Figure 2. Skeleton (3D Model by Thomas Baier)

Chapter 1. Reciprocating Motion

We will discuss some general aspects of general 3D rendering, but our primary focus in this text will be implementation within the context of OpenGL® on the Windows® operating system. For additional details and more specifics, refer to my text, *3D Rendering in Windows*, available from Amazon. The organization of this book is as follows: Specific material of increasing complexity is presented in the chapters, while foundational material (such as rendering contexts) is covered in the appendices.

Miniature Steam Engine Example

In this chapter we will consider one of the most basic forms of articulation: reciprocating motion (i.e., that of a cylinder fitted with a piston connected to a crankshaft). For this we will use a modified version of Troy Robinette's Miniature Steam Engine model, which uses Mark J. Kilgard's GLUT library. We covered this model in book one of this series.

There we were primarily interested in simplicity and, thus, relied heavily on the GLUT library for rendering and program control. Here we will be more interested in the specifics of rendering and also interactivity through the Windows message loop. To that end, we have made several modifications to the original code, including: removing all references to the GLUT library and relying solely on the OpenGL API; eliminating the superfluous texture; eliminating the lists (these are all simple geometric shapes and do not warrant building special rendering lists); use of standard variable types (BOOL, int, float, double, etc.) and minimization of special variable types (GLshort, GLint, GLfloat, GLdouble, etc.).

To improve readability and consistency with the OpenGL API and also the Windows API, function names are like: DrawPiston(), while variable names are like crank_angle. The original version can be found in archive accompanying my previous book. The modified version in examples\steam.

Windows Interface

Before we dive into the rendering, we will consider the Windows interface, which might be thought of as a shell to facilitate the rendering. All Windows programs have the same basic structure. The entry point (code address where the O/S jumps to after having loaded the program into memory) is WinMain(). For a console application (often mistakenly called a DOS box), the entry point is simply main(). These are not optional and are hard-wired into the linker.

WinMain is passed the current and any previous instance (handle to the process assigned by the O/S) and also the command line (launch arguments, such as if you were to *drop* a file onto the executable). The command line has already been parsed into individual strings and stored in the following external variables along with the environment strings:

1

```
extern int __argc;
extern char**__argv;
extern char**_environ;
```

We do not use these externals in this particular example but they are always available and often useful. WinMain performs those tasks necessary for a Windows program to operate. This includes defining objects and procedures followed by a message loop, which will be executed until the program stops. Windows is a message-based O/S, which sends and receives messages for everything that happens. WinMain must also set up the OpenGL rendering context and link this to one or more windows, where the drawing will occur.

```
int WINAPI WinMain(HINSTANCE hCurrent,HINSTANCE
    hPrevious,char*lCommand,int nShow)
  {
  HACCEL acc;
  MSG msg;
  hInst=hCurrent;
  InitCommonControls();
  acc=LoadAccelerators(hInst,"FAST");
  LoadResources();
  RegisterClasses();
  CreateWindows();
  PositionWindows();
  OpenGL();
  SetTimer(hMain,1,10,(TIMERPROC)Animate);
  while(GetMessage(&msg,NULL,0,0))
     if(!TranslateAccelerator(msg.hwnd,acc,&msg))
        if(!TranslateMessage(&msg))
           DispatchMessage(&msg);
  return(0);
  }
```

InitCommonControls() must be called in order to use any of these stock items, which include: status bar, tabs, progress bar, tree view, tool bar, track bar, etc. Here we use the status bar at the bottom of the main windows to display the camera and lighting variables. Accelerators (a list of enhanced keystrokes and corresponding commands) facilitate the use of directional keys and more. One or more resources are also loaded at this point. In this case, the OpenGL logo as a bitmap.

After registering classes, creating and positioning windows (including buttons), initializing the rendering context, we create a timer to facilitate animation, and finally enter the message loop. Messages are received from the O/S through GetMessage(). If it is one of the special accelerator keystrokes, that is translated and dispatched. If not, all other messages are translated and dispatched if relevant. The message loop is ended by a null message, upon which WinMain returns a zero to the O/S, which terminates the program.

2

Windows classes have nothing to do with classes in C++. Windows classes are user-defined procedures that can be called by the O/S upon certain events. There must always be a main procedure, MainProc(), not to be confused with WinMain(). For this example, we also create a procedure to paint the OpenGL logo into the frame, LogoProc(), and one to receive the OpenGL rendering, PlotProc(). The classes are registered by:

```
void RegisterClasses()
  {
  Register("MAIN",MainProc,StockBrush(COLOR_BTNFACE),
    IDC_ARROW,0,0);
  Register("LOGO",LogoProc,StockBrush(COLOR_BTNFACE),
    IDC_ARROW,0,0);
  Register("PLOT",PlotProc,GetStockObject(NULL_BRUSH),
    IDC_CROSS,0,CS_OWNDC);
  }
```

The PLOT window is assigned its own device context to speed drawing by specifying class style CS_OWNDC. Each class is registered by:

```
void Register(char*cName,void*wProc,HBRUSH
    hBrush,char*dCursor,int iExtra,DWORD style)
  {
  WNDCLASS wc;
  memset(&wc,0,sizeof(WNDCLASS));
  wc.hInstance    =hInst;
  wc.hIcon        =LoadIcon(hInst,"ICON");
  wc.style        =CS_HREDRAW|CS_VREDRAW|style;
  wc.lpszClassName=cName;
  wc.lpfnWndProc  =(WNDPROC)wProc;
  wc.hbrBackground=hBrush;
  wc.hCursor      =LoadCursor(NULL,dCursor);
  wc.cbWndExtra   =iExtra;
  if(!RegisterClass(&wc))
    Abort(__LINE__,"can't register '%s' class\nWindows
    error code %i",cName,GetLastError());
  }
```

Windows and associated objects (push buttons, radio buttons, etc.) are created as with any other Windows program. The OpenGL context is initialized by the following code:

```
void OpenGL()
  {
  HGLRC rDC;
  if((pDC=GetBestPixelFormat(hPlot))==0)
    Abort(__LINE__,"can't find best pixel
    context\nWindows error code %i",GetLastError());
  if((rDC=wglCreateContext(pDC))==0)
    Abort(__LINE__,"can't create OpenGL context\nWindows
    error code %i",GetLastError());
```

3

```
if(!wglMakeCurrent(pDC,rDC))
    Abort(__LINE__,"can't make OpenGL context
    current\nWindows error code %i",GetLastError());
    glRepaint();
}
```

This begins with selecting a pixel context (see Appendix A), creating the context, making and the context current. Optionally, the scene may now be painted for the first time. Painting the scene before this will not be successful.

Animation

In a Windows program, animation consists of two parts: creating a timer (which will be called at regular intervals) and providing a procedure. This can be handled in one of two ways. If a separate function is provided, the name of the function is passed as an argument in the timer creation call. If no function is provided (a NULL address is passed in the timer creation call), the WM_TIMER message is sent to the procedure associated with the specified handle (in this hMain), which will then imply MainProc(). The timer is set up by the call:

```
SetTimer(hMain,1,10,(TIMERPROC)Animate);
```

The animation timer for this example is listed below:

```
void WINAPI Animate(HWND hWnd,WPARAM wParam,DWORD
    idEvent,int uTime)
{
if(!animate)
    return;
if(waits)
    {
    waits--;
    return;
    }
crank_angle+=crank_step;
if(crank_angle>360)
    crank_angle=0;
waits=ticks;
glRepaint();
}
```

In order to vary the speed, the procedure counts down (i.e., *waits*) a variable number of *ticks* before changing and redrawing. The only change for this example is the crank angle, which is stepped through 360° by increments of 5°.

Redraw Everything

The default way of creating an animation using OpenGL is to redraw everything. While it is possible to erase part of the *screen* that is in memory (tied to the device context within rendering engine) and repaint only a part of the whole scene, there is no convenient way of doing this or deciding which objects might obscure others. Fortunately, the rendering engine is fast enough to provide acceptable results for even somewhat complex scenes. The *flicker* effect is rarely a problem because OpenGL renders the scene first in memory and then BitBlt's it into the *plot* window.

The rendering process begins with clearing with glClear(), setting up the lighting, shading, camera, and viewing context. The objects are then rendered in any order. The rendering process ends with glFinish(). The BitBlt is accomplished with a call to SwapBuffers().

```
void glRepaint()
{
  if(!pDC)
    return;
  glClearColor(0,0,0,0);
  glClear(GL_COLOR_BUFFER_BIT|GL_DEPTH_BUFFER_BIT);
  glEnable(GL_DEPTH_TEST);
  glDepthFunc(GL_LESS);
  glShadeModel(GL_SMOOTH);
  glLightModeli(GL_LIGHT_MODEL_TWO_SIDE,TRUE);
  glDisable(GL_AUTO_NORMAL);
  glMatrixMode(GL_MODELVIEW);
  glLoadIdentity();
  glEnable(GL_LIGHTING);
  glLightfv(GL_LIGHT0,GL_AMBIENT ,ambientLight0);
  glLightfv(GL_LIGHT0,GL_DIFFUSE ,diffuseLight0);
    positionLight0[0]=(float)(sin(PI*Light.a/180)
      *cos(PI*Light.b/180));
    positionLight0[1]=(float)(sin(PI*Light.b/180));
    positionLight0[2]=(float)(cos(PI*Light.a/180)
      *cos(PI*Light.b/180));
    positionLight0[3]=0;
  glLightfv(GL_LIGHT0,GL_POSITION,positionLight0);
  glEnable(GL_LIGHT0);
  glDisable(GL_TEXTURE_2D);
  glTranslated(Objective.x,Objective.y,Objective.z);
  glRotated(Objective.a,1,0,0);
  glRotated(Objective.b,0,1,0);
  glRotated(Objective.c,0,0,1);
  glPolygonMode(back?GL_FRONT_AND_BACK:GL_FRONT,
    fill?GL_FILL:GL_LINE);
  glScaled(zoom/2.,zoom/2.,zoom/2.);
  RenderEngine();
  glFinish();
  SwapBuffers(pDC);
}
```

Everything up to RenderEngine() is preparation. The two calls after RenderEngine() complete the process. In this case, all of the objects are drawn inside procedure RenderEngine(). This too is broken up into smaller tasks as listed below:

5

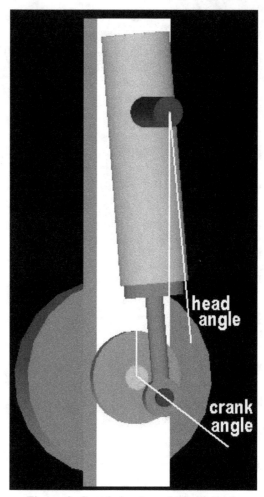

Figure 3. Crank Angle and Head Angle

```
void RenderEngine()
  {
  head_angle=HeadAngle(crank_angle);
  DrawEnginePole();
  glPushMatrix();
  glTranslated(0.5,1.4,0.0);
  DrawCylinderHead();
  glPopMatrix();
  glPushMatrix();
  glTranslated(0.0,-0.8,0.0);
  DrawCrank();
  glPopMatrix();
```

6

}
The crank angle is updated in the animation procedure and the head angle is calculated once here to complete the arrangement. This formula can be found on the Web along with a description of reciprocating systems. The formula is provided as a function:

```
double HeadAngle(double deg)
{
double theta;
theta=270.112-deg/58.;
return(120.*atan((0.15*sin(theta))/
        ((2.7-0.15*cos(theta))))));
}
```

The individual parts are broken down into simple geometric shapes (block, cylinder, and disk):

```
void DrawPiston()
{
glPushMatrix();
glColor(0.3F,0.6F,0.9F);
glPushMatrix();
glRotated(90.,0.0,1.0,0.0);
glTranslated(0.0,0.0,-0.07);
glShaft(0.125,0.06,0.12);
glPopMatrix();
glRotated(-90.,1.0,0.0,0.0);
glTranslated(0.0,0.0,0.05);
glShaft(0.06,0.0,0.6);
glTranslated(0.0,0.0,0.6);
glShaft(0.2,0.0,0.5);
glPopMatrix();
}
void DrawEnginePole()
{
glPushMatrix();
glColor(0.9F,0.9F,0.9F);
glBox(0.5,3.0,0.5);
glColor(0.5F,0.1F,0.5F);
glRotated(90.,0.0,1.0,0.0);
glTranslated(0.0,0.9,-0.4);
glShaft(0.1,0.0,2);
glPopMatrix();
}
void DrawCylinderHead()
{
glPushMatrix();
glColor(0.5F,1.0F,0.5F);
glRotated(90.,1.0,0.0,0.0);
glTranslated(0,0.0,0.4);
```

7

```
    glRotated(head_angle,1,0,0);
    glTranslated(0,0.0,-0.4);
    glShaft(0.23,0.21,1.6);
    glRotated(180.,1.0,0.0,0.0);
    glRing(0.,0.23,20);
    glPopMatrix();
}
void DrawFlywheel()
{
    glPushMatrix();
    glColor(0.5F,0.5F,1.0F);
    glRotated(90.,0.0,1.0,0.0);
    glShaft(0.625,0.08,0.5);
    glPopMatrix();
}
void DrawCrankbell()
{
    glPushMatrix();
    glColor(1.0F,0.5F,0.5F);
    glRotated(90.,0.0,1.0,0.0);
    glShaft(0.3,0.08,0.12);
    glColor(0.5F,0.1F,0.5F);
    glTranslated(0.0,0.2,0.0);
    glShaft(0.06,0.0,0.34);
    glTranslated(0.0,0.0,0.22);
    glRotated(90.,0.0,1.0,0.0);
    glRotated(crank_angle-head_angle,1.0,0.0,0.0);
    DrawPiston();
    glPopMatrix();
}
void DrawCrank()
{
    glPushMatrix();
    glRotated(crank_angle,1.0,0.0,0.0);
    glPushMatrix();
    glRotated(90.,0.0,1.0,0.0);
    glTranslated(0.0,0.0,-1.0);
    glShaft(0.08,0.0,1.4);
    glPopMatrix();
    glPushMatrix();
    glTranslated(0.28,0.0,0.0);
    DrawCrankbell();
    glPopMatrix();
    glPushMatrix();
    glTranslated(-0.77,0.0,0.0);
    DrawFlywheel();
    glPopMatrix();
    glPopMatrix();
}
```

These individual procedures further break down the drawing process to generic geometric objects. Rather than drawing an arbitrary hexahedron at some particular location and orientation, it is simpler to modify the transformation matrix through which all objects pass and draw a generic object. In order to preserve the transformation within the rendering context, we first save it with glPushMatrix(), perform the desired actions, and then restore it with glPopMatrix().

Not only does this simplify the basic drawing functions, it also facilitates debugging. We know that the generic objects will be drawn correctly. If the final objects are not rendered as desired, the problem must be in the preparation (rotate, translate, scale, etc.) or preservation (push, draw, pop). This sequence and program structure, including separating those procedures unique to Windows from those pertaining to OpenGL makes the code more understandable.

Degrees of Freedom

This example essentially has only one degree of freedom: crank angle. The head angle is uniquely defined by the linkage from the crank angle and so it is not independent. There are also only a few objects impacted by changing the crank angle. Rotation, scaling, lighting, etc. are merely viewing aspects and not articulations. This is perhaps the simplest system of the type covered in this text.

Animation Rate

Live animation rate is limited by the time to render and paint and also process messages. These are not optional steps and would be present in most any O/S and certainly any multi-user or multi-processing system. If the rate is insufficient, the only practical remedy is screen capture and building an animated file, such as a GIF.

Chapter 2. Simple Leg Motion

For this next example we will begin Brian Paul's Blue Pony example, which also utilizes the GLUT library. In order to focus on the leg motion alone, we will eliminate the billboard logo, replacing it with a red panel. This eliminates the texture reading, conversion, and drawing code, as this does not contribute to our discussion of articulation. The original code uses 2D polygons to define the parts of the pony (body, mane, and legs). These were first tessellated (converted to triangles) and then extruded (to provide thickness). As these operations rely on the GLUT library and are not directly related to articulation, the pony will be transformed into 3D triangles, which are easily drawn. This operation was performed externally and the results stored in a static data statement (see file pony.3dv in folder examples\pony). For more details on working with finite elements, refer to the previous two texts.

Figure 4. Pony Example (solid)

We will also replace the dependence on the GLUT library with foundational calls to the OpenGL API alone. Finally, we will replace the original GUI functions (also from the GLUT library) with Windows API calls, as with the steam engine in Chapter 1. In fact, the user interface, program control, and message loop will be identical to the previous one. Even the animation procedure will be the same so that the only difference between the two will be replacing RenderEngine() with RenderPony(). The triangles can be seen in the wire frame view.

Figure 5. Pony Example (wire frame)

There are only two leg objects (front and rear). Each is drawn twice. The lateral displacement is always the same. The rotating motion is implemented by calling glRotatef() and passing the leg rotation angle, which is incremented as before with the crank angle. There is very little difference between the pony and steam engine examples—mostly the shape of the objects.

```
void RenderPony()
    {
    glColor(0.1F,0.1F,1.0F);
    glTriangles(body);
    glColor(1.0F,0.5F,0.5F);
    glTriangles(mane);
```

12

```
glColor(0.1F,0.1F,1.0F);
glPushMatrix();
glTranslatef(FrontLegPos[0],FrontLegPos[1],
  FrontLegPos[2]);
glRotatef(LegAngle,0.0,0.0,1.0);
glTriangles(fleg);
glPopMatrix();
glPushMatrix();
glTranslatef(FrontLegPos[0],FrontLegPos[1],
  -FrontLegPos[2]);
glRotatef(-LegAngle,0.0,0.0,1.0);
glTriangles(fleg);
glPopMatrix();
glPushMatrix();
glTranslatef(BackLegPos[0],BackLegPos[1],
  BackLegPos[2]);
glRotatef(-LegAngle,0.0,0.0,1.0);
glTriangles(rleg);
glPopMatrix();
glPushMatrix();
glTranslatef(BackLegPos[0],BackLegPos[1],
  -BackLegPos[2]);
glRotatef(LegAngle,0.0,0.0,1.0);
glTriangles(rleg);
glPopMatrix();
}
```

Chapter 3. Walking Motion

We next discuss walking motion. Our example, of course, will be an Imperial Walker. Before we can delve into articulating each leg, we must first identify the various parts, including the joints. These have been separated by colors in the figure below (author unknown):

Figure 6. Parts of an Imperial Walker

You can readily find such models on the Web. These are usually in the form of VRML (Virtual Reality Markup Language) files or 3DS (AutoCAD® 3D Studio) files, which are rather inconvenient to work with unless you have very expensive software. These can be translated by TP2 (see Appendix C) into 3D elements or triangles, both simple text files that are convenient to work with (see pony.3dv and pony.tri in the Chapter 2). There are several file conversions (with source code) available in the utilities folder in the online archive. Separating out one leg, we see the details, including the points of rotation shown in red:

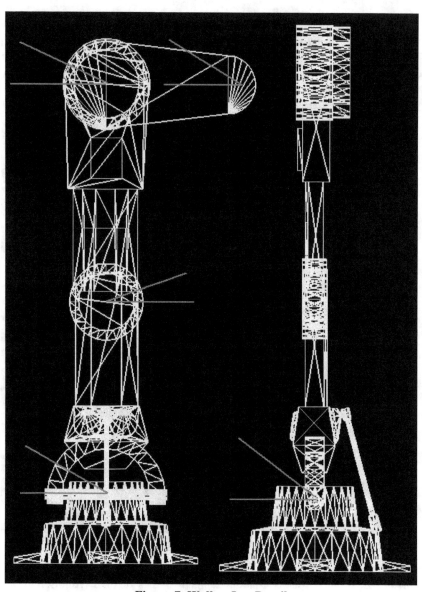

Figure 7. Walker Leg Detail

As with the steam engine and pony, we will first draw the parts that do not articulate, then apply appropriate translations and rotations (pushing the transformation onto the stack before and popping it off the stack afterward) draw a group of elements, then move on to the next group. In order for the hip joint to work properly, we must rotate two groups by equal and opposite angles and also displace the second, as shown below:

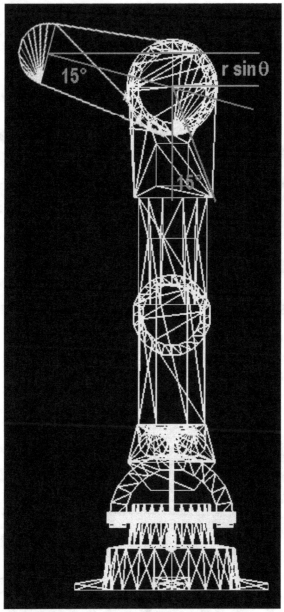

Figure 8. Hip Joint Rotation/Displacement Detail

The left, right, front, and rear legs can be drawn from the same group of elements with rotation and translation. First we split the legs into sections.

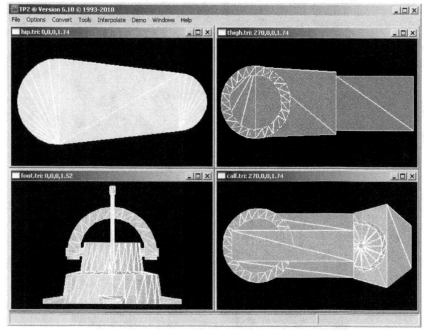

Figure 9. Walker Leg Split into 4 Groups

If the groups are not obvious from the source file (for example, 3DS or VRML), you can select individual elements with TP2 and split the groups manually. To do this, load the file and then select the option *selection of 3D objects*. When you click on each element, it will change colors. The default new color is red but you can change it with the *selection color* option.

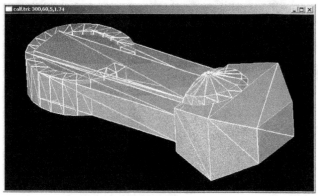

Figure 10. Walker Calf Group

You may also want to outline the elements. To do this, select *User Controls* from the *Windows* menu, as shown below. You can also use the controls to pan and adjust the view.

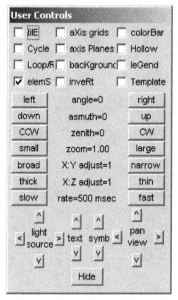

Figure 11. TP2 User Controls

In order to further discuss these groups, we will bring them into Excel® where they can be rotated and translated using simple functions. You will find two programs (3DVtoCSV and TRItoCSV) to facilitate this process in the utilities folder. Comma Separated Values (CSV) can be opened by Excel® and are a native format. Each of the element groups forming the leg has been converted to comma separated values and combined into a single spreadsheet, walker.xls that you will find in the examples\walker folder.

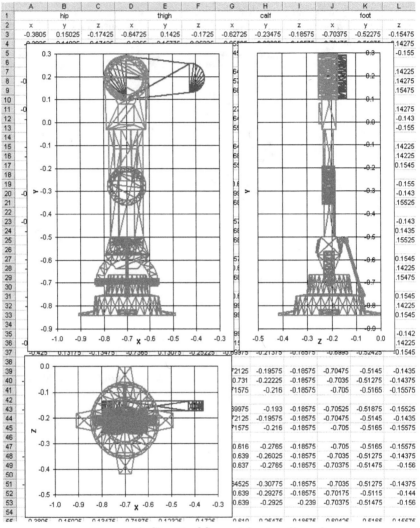

Figure 12. Sheet1 of Spreadsheet walker.xls

Rotations are most efficiently performed using matrix operations. These are covered in Chapter 3 of *3D Rendering in Windows* in more detail and are implemented in Sheet2 of the spreadsheet walker.xls over to the right side, as shown in this next figure. The user-adjustable angles are in bold blue font.

20

M	N	O
5	x-rotation	
1	0	0
0	0.996195	-0.08716
0	0.087156	0.996195
10	y-rotation	
0.984808	0	0.173648
0	1	0
-0.17365	0	0.984808
15	z-rotation	
0.965926	-0.25882	0
0.258819	0.965926	0
0	0	1
combined rotation		
0.951251	-0.25489	0.173648
0.272453	0.958333	-0.08583
-0.14454	0.128958	0.98106

Figure 13. Rotation Matrices

Rotations about the three axes (xyz) are specified by three angles $(\theta\varphi\psi)$ using the following three 3x3 matrices, one at a time. A rotation about the x-axis by an angle θ is performed by the following matrix operation:

$$\begin{vmatrix} 1 & 0 & 0 \\ 0 & \cos\theta & -\sin\theta \\ 0 & \sin\theta & \cos\theta \end{vmatrix} \quad (3.1)$$

A rotation about the y-axis by an angle φ is performed by the following matrix operation:

$$\begin{vmatrix} \cos\varphi & 0 & \sin\varphi \\ 0 & 1 & 0 \\ -\sin\varphi & 0 & \cos\varphi \end{vmatrix} \quad (3.2)$$

A rotation about the z-axis by an angle ψ is performed by the following matrix operation:

$$\begin{vmatrix} \cos\psi & -\sin\psi & 0 \\ \sin\psi & \cos\psi & 0 \\ 0 & 0 & 1 \end{vmatrix} \quad (3.3)$$

The three rotations are combined using two calls to the Excel® matrix multiplication function (MMULT):

```
=MMULT(MMULT(M2:O4,M6:O8),M10:O12)
```

21

The rotation is applied using one call to MMULT and two calls to the transpose function (TRANSPOSE):

```
=TRANSPOSE(MMULT($M$14:$O$16,TRANSPOSE(Sheet1!A3:C3)))
```

The end result for $\theta=5°$, $\varphi=10°$, and $\psi=15°$ is:

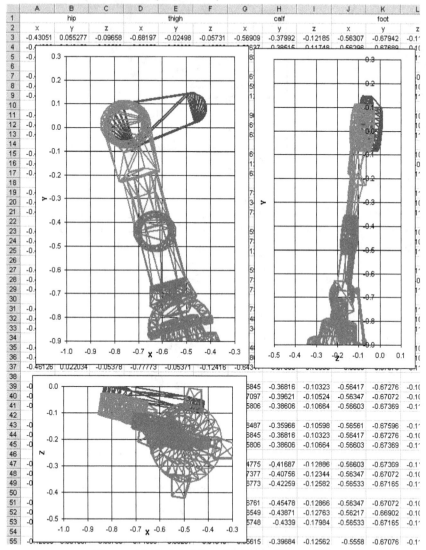

Figure 14. Rotated Leg ($\theta=5°$, $\varphi=10°$, $\psi=15°$)

We start with the same basic program as in the pony example, only we read the walker elements from walker.tri, as shown in the next figure:

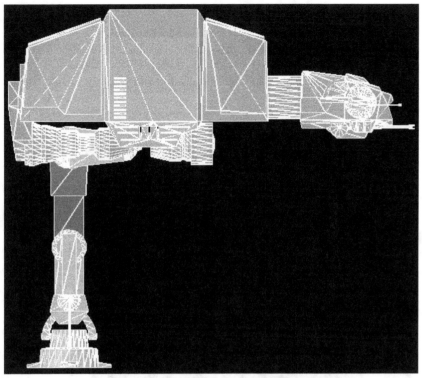

Figure 15. One-Legged Model in 3D Triangles

Rendering the entire walker using only one leg four times requires only a short section of code. The four data statements (dX,dZ,dW,yA) contain the adjustments to make 4 legs out of 1 group of elements.

```
void RenderWalker()
  {
  int i;
  float dX[4]={0.F,0.000F,-0.473F,-0.473F};
  float dZ[4]={0.F,0.309F, 0.000F,-0.309F};
  float dW[4]={0.F,0.423F, 0.000F,-0.423F};
  float yA[4]={0.F,0.F,180.F,180.F};
  glColor(1.F,0.F,0.F);
  glTriangles(body);
  for(i=0;i<4;i++)
    {
    glPushMatrix();
    glTranslatef(dX[i],0.F,dZ[i]);
    glRotatef(yA[i],0.F,1.F,0.F);
    glColor(0.F,1.F,1.F);
    glTriangles(hip);
    glPopMatrix();
```

23

```
glPushMatrix();
glTranslatef(dX[i],0.F,dW[i]);
glRotatef(yA[i],0.F,1.F,0.F);
glColor(0.F,1.F,1.F);
glColor(0.F,1.F,0.F);
glTriangles(thigh);
glColor(1.F,1.F,0.F);
glTriangles(calf);
glColor(0.F,1.F,0.F);
glTriangles(foot);
glPopMatrix();
  }
}
```

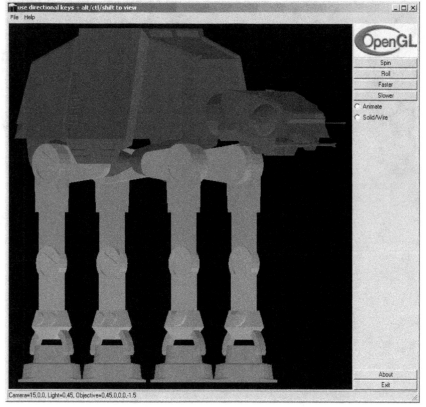

Figure 16. Assembled Walker

<u>Hip Rotation</u>

The cyan hip groups are rotated by some angle (Ahip), which can be different for each of the four hips. As each hip rotates through some angle, the group must be repositioned so as to maintain the pivot location on the body. The X and Y adjustments are given by:

```
hX=0.465*(cos((Ahip- 25)*PI/180)-cos( -25*PI/180));
hY=0.465*(cos((Ahip-115)*PI/180)-cos(-115*PI/180));
```

The inner radius is 0.465, the point of maximum horizontal displacement is 25°, and the point of maximum vertical displacement is 115°. This radius and angle come from the vector from the centroid (X=Y=Z) and the pivot point of the hip at the center of the smaller end that attaches to the body.

Thigh Rotation

The thigh group must be adjusted so that it follows the larger end of the hip as it rotates. The radius (0.275) is the distance between the two round sections on either end of the hip.

```
pX= 0.275*(cos(Ahip*PI/180)-1);
pY=-0.275* sin(Ahip*PI/180);
```

Rotating the thigh group produces displacements, which must be compensated for if the outer (second) hip joint is to remain intact. The radius (0.728) and angle (286°) arises from the vector between the centroid and knee.

```
tX= 0.728*(sin((Athigh-286)*PI/180)-sin(-286*PI/180));
tY=-0.728*(cos((Athigh-286)*PI/180)-cos(-286*PI/180));
```

We can assign a pair of keys to the hip and thigh rotation angles to conveniently control the display groups. Rotating the hips +90° and the thighs -90° produces the following:

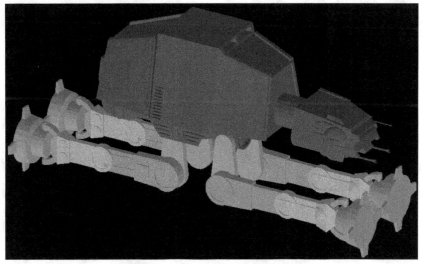

Figure 17. Hips +90° and Thighs -90°

25

Calf Rotation

The calf group must be adjusted so that it follows the lower thigh joint. Note that our rotations control the segments, not the joints. The thigh rotation angle doesn't impact the knee per se in this model because the joints are simple disks. It does, however, impact the calf group, which will require a rotation and two displacements, as before so that the knee joint remains intact. The radius is 0.753 and the angle is 249°.

```
cX= 0.753*(sin((Acalf-249)*PI/180)-sin(-249*PI/180));
cY=-0.753*(cos((Acalf-249)*PI/180)-cos(-249*PI/180));
```

Foot Rotation

And finally, the foot position must be adjusted to keep the ankle joint together. This is accomplished by the following code. The radius is 0.928 and the angle is 229°.

```
fX= 0.928*(sin((Afoot-229)*PI/180)-sin(-229*PI/180));
fY=-0.928*(cos((Afoot-229)*PI/180)-cos(-229*PI/180));
```

As we have assigned each of these angles a hot key (hip=CTL_UP/DOWN, thigh=CTL_LEFT/RIGHT, calf=ALT_PGUP/DN, foot=CTL_PGUP/DN), we can move the legs interactively.

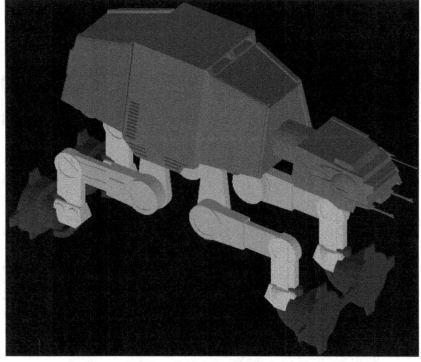

Figure 18. Hip=Calf=90° and Thigh=Foot=-90°

26

The interactive adjustments are simple, as illustrated by the following:

```
if(wParam==PUSH_CTL_DOWN)
  {
  Ahip[0]+=5.F;
  Ahip[1]+=5.F;
  Ahip[2]+=5.F;
  Ahip[3]+=5.F;
  glRepaint();
  return(TRUE);
  }
```

Coordinated Leg Motion

In order to achieve coordinated leg motion, we must vary the for angles for each leg separately over time. To do this, we merely set up a table that goes through a cycle consisting of one stride for a single leg. Each leg will go through the same motions, only there will be a time delay between each. Conceptually, this looks like the figure below:

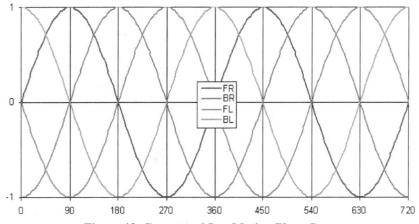

Figure 19. Conceptual Leg Motion Phase Lags

This pattern is easily implemented by a snippet of code:

```
Twalk+=5.;
for(i=0;i<4;i++)
  {
  Ahip[  i]=-(10* sin((Twalk-i*90)*PI/180)-5 );
  Athigh[i]= (20*(cos((Twalk-i*90)*PI/180)-1));
  Acalf[ i]= (20* cos((Twalk-i*90)*PI/180)  );
  Afoot[ i]=-Athigh[i]-Acalf[i];
  }
```

More complex patterns can be implemented in a similar fashion. One might even provide multiple gaits (walk, trot, canter, gallop). For this particular linkage, setting Afoot+Athigh+Acalf=0 will keep the foot parallel to the ground.

27

The animation is progressed by simply incrementing the sequence angle, Twalk. The phase angle between the legs progressively lags by 90° (-i*90). More complicated sequences are, of course, possible. To conceptualize and implement more complex motions, it is often helpful to construct a physical model of the linkage, as illustrated below:

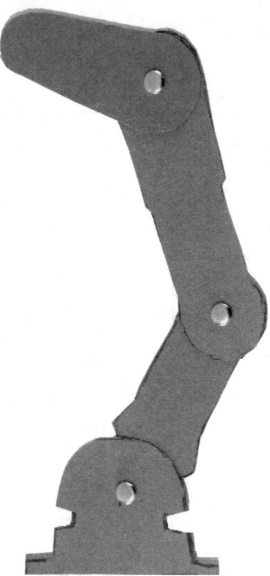

Figure 20. Adjustable Cardboard Leg Model

And finally, we have the walker galloping along at the touch of a button:

Figure 21. Walker Complete with Animation

Chapter 4. Skeletal Motion

The skeleton model (shown on page iv) was obtained from the Web, written in #VRML V2.0 by Thomas Baier (thomas.baier@stmuc.com) dated Apr 03 10:14:40 2002. We first break it up into groups and write these out as 3D triangles using wrlto3dv and 3dvtotri, which may be found in the utilities folder in the online archive accompanying this text. The end result can be displayed using TP2:

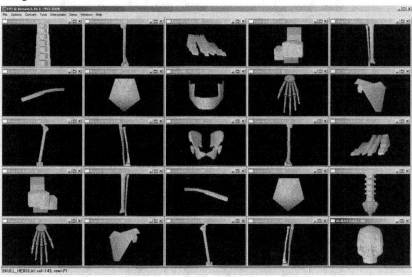

Figure 22. Skeletal Groups

There were only 5 groups to the walker (body, hip, thigh, calf, and foot) and so we had a separate section of code to read each one. There are 26 groups in the skeleton, which warrants a more flexible arrangement and referencing. One way to do this is with an index, which indicates the beginning of each group. The length of each group is the difference between the beginning of the group and the beginning of the next group. We can also assign an index to each group and use this to reference them. C will automatically assign indices:

```
enum{skull,mandible,cervneck,thorax,lclavicl,lscapula,
   lhumerus,llarm,lhand,rclavicl,rscapula,rhumerus,
   rlarm,rhand,pelvis,saclumbr,lfemur,lknee,llleg,
   lfoot,ltoes,rfemur,rknee,rlleg,rfoot,rtoes};
```

The model is stored in the following structure:

```
typedef struct{float x,y,z;}XYZ;
typedef struct{XYZ c,n,p,q,r;}TRI;
struct{int*i,n;TRI*t;}model;
```

The basic model is shown below in solid and wire frame:

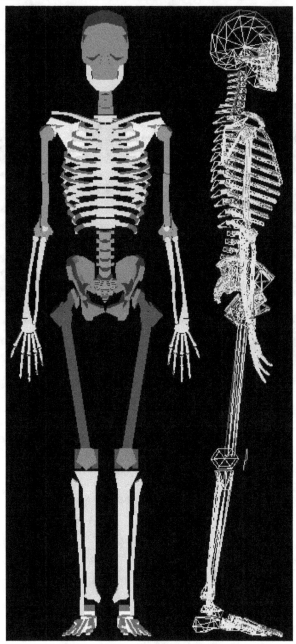

Figure 23. Basic Skeleton Model

The model is rendered by group, as shown below (before adding rotations for simplification):

```
void RenderSkeleton()
  {
  int g,n;
  float red[3]={1.F,0.F,0.F};
  float green[3]={0.F,1.F,0.F};
  TRI t;
  for(g=0;g<=rtoes;g++)
    {
    for(n=model.i[g];n<model.i[g+1];n++)
      {
      t=model.t[n];
      if(group<0)
        glMaterialfv(fill?GL_FRONT_AND_BACK:GL_FRONT,
          GL_AMBIENT_AND_DIFFUSE,(float*)&t.c);
      else if(g==group)
        glMaterialfv(fill?GL_FRONT_AND_BACK:GL_FRONT,
          GL_AMBIENT_AND_DIFFUSE,red);
      else
        glMaterialfv(fill?GL_FRONT_AND_BACK:GL_FRONT,
          GL_AMBIENT_AND_DIFFUSE,green);
      glBegin(GL_POLYGON);
      glNormal3f(t.n.x,t.n.y,t.n.z);
      glVertex3f(t.p.x,t.p.y,t.p.z);
      glVertex3f(t.q.x,t.q.y,t.q.z);
      glVertex3f(t.r.x,t.r.y,t.r.z);
      glEnd();
      }
    }
  }
```

Here we can color normally or make one group a different color (red) from all the rest (green). The group can be selected with a pair of hot keys:

```
if(wParam==PUSH_ALT_SPACE)
  {
  group--;
  if(group<-1)
    group=rtoes;
  glRepaint();
  return(TRUE);
  }
if(wParam==PUSH_CTL_SPACE)
  {
  group++;
  if(group>rtoes)
    group=-1;
  glRepaint();
  return(TRUE);
```

}

The figure below shows the thorax red and the rest green:

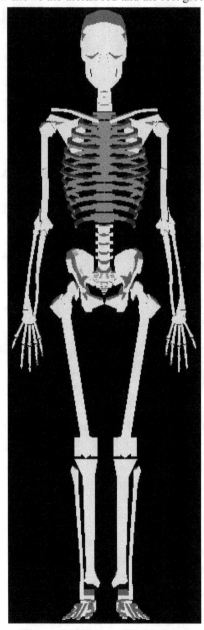

Figure 24. Thorax Highlighted

Simply hold down CTL or ALT and tap the spacebar to cycle through the groups. This illustrates how to add interactive features and also helps in formulating the articulation equations.

Shoulder Rotation

We assign the left and right shoulder rotations to hot keys alt-S and ctl-S, respectively .the shoulder vector is 25.35 in length at 91° making the corresponding adjustments:

```
if(g==lhumerus||g==llarm||g==lhand)
{
R=25.35;
A=91.;
dX=0.;
dY=( R*(sin((lShoulder-A)*PI/180)
-sin(-A*PI/180))));
dZ=(-R*(cos((lShoulder-A)*PI/180)
  -cos(-A*PI/180))));
glTranslatef(dX,dY,dZ);
glRotatef(lShoulder,1.F,0.F,0.F);
}
if(g==rhumerus||g==rlarm||g==rhand)
{
R=25.35;
A=91.;
dX=0.;
dY=( R*(sin((rShoulder-A)*PI/180)
  -sin(-A*PI/180))));
dZ=(-R*(cos((rShoulder-A)*PI/180)
  -cos(-A*PI/180))));
glTranslatef(dX,dY,dZ);
glRotatef(rShoulder,1.F,0.F,0.F);
}
```

Note that we must apply these same adjustments to the lower arm and hand, as they are connected to the humerus.

Elbow Adjustments

In order to keep the elbow joint intact, we must adjust all of the groups attached to the humerus. The elbow vector is 11.8 in length and 93° making the corresponding adjustments:

```
if(g==llarm||g==lhand)
{
R=11.8;
A=93.;
dX=0.;
dY=( R*(sin((lElbow-A)*PI/180)-sin(-A*PI/180)));
dZ=(-R*(cos((lElbow-A)*PI/180)-cos(-A*PI/180)));
glTranslatef(dX,dY,dZ);
glRotatef(lElbow,1.F,0.F,0.F);
```

```
    }
if(g==rlarm||g==rhand)
{
R=11.8;
A=93.;
dX=0.;
dY=( R*(sin((rElbow-A)*PI/180)-sin(-A*PI/180)));
dZ=(-R*(cos((rElbow-A)*PI/180)-cos(-A*PI/180)));
glTranslatef(dX,dY,dZ);
glRotatef(rElbow,1.F,0.F,0.F);
}
```

Wrist Rotation

The wrist has two degrees of freedom and two rotation angles. We assign the left and right wrist rotations to hot keys alt-R and ctl-R, respectively .The wrist rotation vector is 10.5 in length at 85° making the corresponding adjustments:

```
if(g==lhand)
{
R=10.5;
A=85.;
dX=(R*(sin((LWrist-A)*PI/180)
  -sin(-A*PI/180)));
dY=0.F;
dZ=(R*(cos((LWrist-A)*PI/180)
  -cos(-A*PI/180)));
glTranslatef(dX,dY,dZ);
glRotatef(LWrist,0.F,1.F,0.F);
}
if(g==rhand)
{
R=10.5;
A=-85.;
dX=(R*(sin((-RWrist-A)*PI/180)
  -sin(-A*PI/180)));
dY=0.F;
dZ=(R*(cos((-RWrist-A)*PI/180)
  -cos(-A*PI/180)));
glTranslatef(dX,dY,dZ);
glRotatef(-RWrist,0.F,1.F,0.F);
}
```

We assign the left and right wrist flexing motions to hot keys alt-F and ctl-F, respectively .The wrist flex vector is 1.2 in length at 0° making the corresponding adjustments (same right and left):

```
dY=-R*(sin((rWristF-A)*PI/180)-sin(-A*PI/180));
dZ= R*(cos((rWristF-A)*PI/180)-cos(-A*PI/180));
glTranslatef(0.F,dY,dZ);
glRotatef(rWristF,1.F,0.F,0.F);
```

We can now position both arms and hands with combinations of ctl/alt SERF, as illustrated in this next figure:

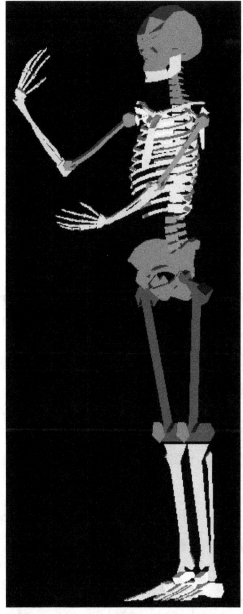

Figure 25. Arm and Hand Articulation

Jaw Motion

We will assign the alt-J hotkey to move the jaw. The radius in this case is 33.6 (see, for instance, the average Y coordinate in mandible.tri) and the angle is 90°, making the adjustments:

```
if(g==mandible)
  {
  R=33.6;
  A=90.;
  dY= R*(sin((Mandible-A)*PI/180)-sin(-A*PI/180));
  dZ=-R*(cos((Mandible-A)*PI/180)-cos(-A*PI/180));
  glTranslatef(0.F,dY,dZ);
  glRotatef(Mandible,1.F,0.F,0.F);
  }
```

We also limit the rotation from -45° to 0°:

```
if(wParam==PUSH_ALT_J)
  {
  Mandible-=5.F;
  if(Mandible<-44.F)
    Mandible=0.F;
  glRepaint();
  return(TRUE);
  }
```

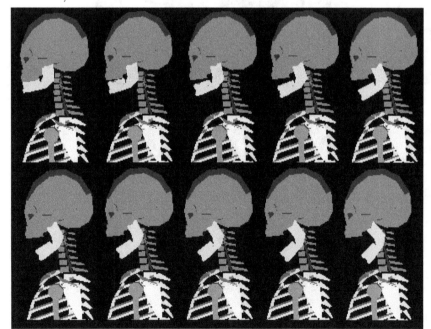

Figure 26. Jaw Rotation

38

Hip Rotation

We assign the hotkeys alt-H and ctl-H to the left and right hip rotation, respectively. The hip vector is 3.6 in length at 120° (see average X value of upper portion in lfemur.tri), making the adjustments:

```
if(g==lfemur||g==lpatella||g==lfibia||g==lfoot
   ||g==ltoes)
{
R=3.6;
A=120.;
dY=( R*(sin((lHip-A)*PI/180)-sin(-A*PI/180)));
dZ=(-R*(cos((lHip-A)*PI/180)-cos(-A*PI/180)));
glTranslatef(0.F,dY,dZ);
glRotatef(lHip,1.F,0.F,0.F);
}
if(g==rfemur||g==rpatella||g==rfibia||g==rfoot
   ||g==rtoes)
{
R=3.6;
A=120.;
dY=( R*(sin((rHip-A)*PI/180)-sin(-A*PI/180)));
dZ=(-R*(cos((rHip-A)*PI/180)-cos(-A*PI/180)));
glTranslatef(0.F,dY,dZ);
glRotatef(rHip,1.F,0.F,0.F);
}
```

We limit the hip rotation to -70° to +110°.

Knee Rotation

We assign the hotkeys alt-K and ctl-K to the left and right knee rotation, respectively. The knee vector is 20 in length at 20° (see average Y value of upper portion in llleg.tri), making the adjustments (same for left and right):

```
if(g==lfibia||g==lfoot||g==ltoes)
{
R=20.;
A=100.;
dY=(-R*(sin((-lKnee-A)*PI/180)-sin(-A*PI/180)));
dZ=( R*(cos((-lKnee-A)*PI/180)-cos(-A*PI/180)));
glTranslatef(0.F,dY,dZ);
glRotatef(-lKnee,1.F,0.F,0.F);
}
```

We limit the knee rotation to 0° to 120°.

Ankle Rotation

We assign the hotkeys alt-A and ctl-A to the left and right ankle rotation, respectively. The ankle vector is 38 in length at 97° (see average Y value of upper portion in llleg.tri), making the adjustments (same for left and right):

```
if(g==lfoot||g==ltoes)
{
```

```
R=38.;
A=97.;
dY=(-R*(sin((lAnkle-A)*PI/180)-sin(-A*PI/180)));
dZ=( R*(cos((lAnkle-A)*PI/180)-cos(-A*PI/180)));
glTranslatef(0.F,dY,dZ);
glRotatef(lAnkle,1.F,0.F,0.F);
}
```

We limit the ankle rotation to -60° to +40°. We can not pose the skeleton as desired using a combination of hot keys.

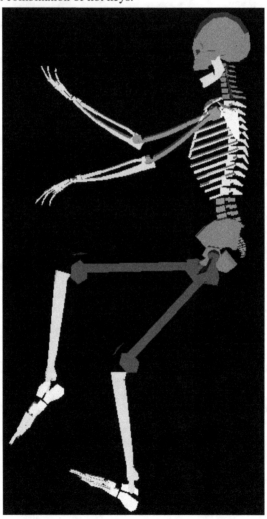

Figure 27. Interactively Posed Skeleton

Walking Motion

We can combine leg (and optionally arm) angles to approximate walking. While we could do something more elaborate, the same sort of algorithm used for the previous walker will do here.

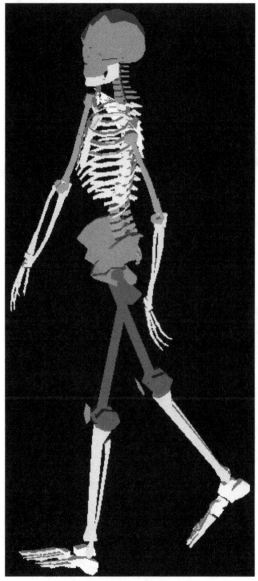

Figure 28. Walking Skeleton

Chapter 5. Rigid Wing Articulation

We will cover wing articulation in two steps: rigid and continuous. As hummingbird wings flex considerably less than all other birds, we will use a hummingbird for this first step. It was simple enough to distinguish between discrete parts of the previous models and identify these with different colors. We will be moving all the elements associated with the wings proportionately. It is more efficient to use nodes and elements than triangles, as the nodes appear in several elements. Displacing them before drawing makes more sense here than using OpenGL calls to perform this operation, as in the previous examples. The hummingbird model is read from humbird.3dv, which is located in the examples folder. A sample is listed below:

```
952 nodes
-0.00313818 -0.0117455 0.0049336
-0.00231971 -0.0114476 0.00516605
-0.00317203 -0.0121183 0.00493927
-0.00353294 -0.012288 0.00481474
-0.00252134 -0.0125129 0.00438231
-0.00354298 -0.0128829 0.00440458
etc.
1900 elements
500 502 501 RGB=0x8C8162
502 503 501 RGB=0xAB9D7B
502 504 503 RGB=0x928768
504 505 503 RGB=0xB09F82
506 505 504 RGB=0xB1A389
506 507 505 RGB=0xB2A48A
etc.
```

The model is read by the following code, which is similar to read3dv.c:

```
void ReadModel(char*fname)
    {
    char bufr[128],*ptr;
    int e,i,j,k,n;
    double x,y,z;
    FILE*fp;
    if((fp=fopen(fname,"rt"))==NULL)
        Abort(__LINE__,"can't open model file: %s",fname);
    if(!fgets(bufr,sizeof(bufr),fp))
        Abort(__LINE__,"unexpected end of file");
    if(sscanf(bufr,"%i",&nodes)!=1)
        Abort(__LINE__,"scan error on number of nodes");
    if(nodes<100)
        Abort(__LINE__,"expected at least 100 nodes but
        found %i",nodes);
    if((Node=calloc(nodes,sizeof(NODE)))==NULL)
        Abort(__LINE__,"can't allocate memory for nodes");
    for(i=0;i<nodes;i++)
        {
```

43

```
     if(!fgets(bufr,sizeof(bufr),fp))
        Abort(__LINE__,"unexpected end of file");
     if(sscanf(bufr,"%lf%*[ ,\t]%lf%*[
,\t]%lf",&x,&y,&z)!=3)
        Abort(__LINE__,"scan error on x,y,z");
     Node[i].x=x;
     Node[i].y=y;
     Node[i].z=z;
     }
  if(!fgets(bufr,sizeof(bufr),fp))
     Abort(__LINE__,"unexpected end of file");
  if(sscanf(bufr,"%i",&elems)!=1)
     Abort(__LINE__,"scan error on number of elements");
  if(elems<100)
     Abort(__LINE__,"expected at least 100 elements but
     found %i",elems);
  if((Elem=calloc(elems,sizeof(ELEM)))==NULL)
     Abort(__LINE__,"can't allocate memory for
     elements");
  for(e=0;e<elems;e++)
     {
     if(!fgets(bufr,sizeof(bufr),fp))
        Abort(__LINE__,"unexpected end of file");
     if(sscanf(bufr,"%i%*[ ,\t]%i%*[
,\t]%i%n",&i,&j,&k,&n)!=3)
        Abort(__LINE__,"scan error on i,j,k");
     if(i<1||i>nodes)
        Abort(__LINE__,"no such node %i",i);
     if(j<1||j>nodes)
        Abort(__LINE__,"no such node %i",j);
     if(k<1||k>nodes)
        Abort(__LINE__,"no such node %i",k);
     Elem[e].i=i-1;
     Elem[e].j=j-1;
     Elem[e].k=k-1;
     ptr=bufr+n;
     while(strchr(" \t,",*ptr))
        ptr++;
     if(_memicmp(ptr,"rgb=",4)==0)
        ptr+=4;
     if(ptr[0]!='0'||ptr[1]!='x')
        Abort(__LINE__,"scan error on 0xRRGGBB following
     i,j,k");
     sscanf(ptr,"%i",&Elem[e].rgb);
     }
  fclose(fp);
  }
```

The GUI and associated procedures and objects are contained in humbird.c and humbird.rc and are similar to the codes for the walker and skeleton.

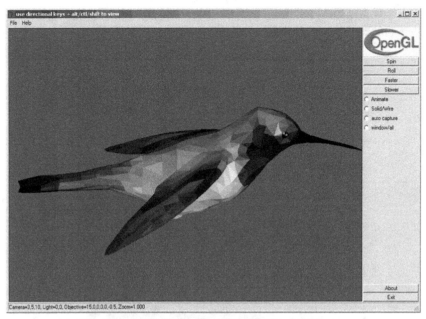

Figure 29. Hummingbird Windows GUI

Figure 30. Hummingbird Wire Frame Elements

45

The hummingbird elements may also be viewed in the Excel spreadsheet humbird.xls, as shown below:

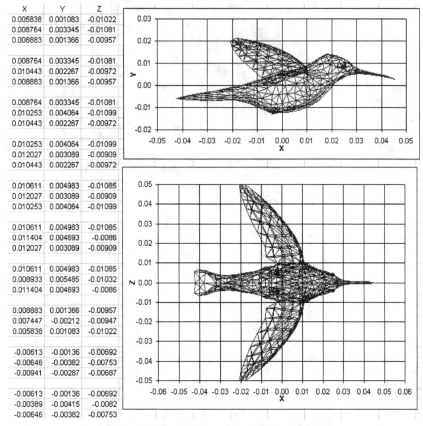

X	Y	Z
0.005838	0.001083	-0.01022
0.008764	0.003345	-0.01081
0.008883	0.001366	-0.00957
0.008764	0.003345	-0.01081
0.010443	0.002267	-0.00972
0.008883	0.001366	-0.00957
0.008764	0.003345	-0.01081
0.010253	0.004064	-0.01099
0.010443	0.002267	-0.00972
0.010253	0.004064	-0.01099
0.012027	0.003089	-0.00909
0.010443	0.002267	-0.00972
0.010611	0.004983	-0.01085
0.012027	0.003089	-0.00909
0.010253	0.004064	-0.01099
0.010611	0.004983	-0.01085
0.011404	0.004693	-0.0086
0.012027	0.003089	-0.00909
0.010611	0.004983	-0.01085
0.008933	0.005485	-0.01032
0.011404	0.004693	-0.0086
0.008883	0.001366	-0.00957
0.007447	-0.00212	-0.00947
0.005838	0.001083	-0.01022
-0.00613	-0.00136	-0.00692
-0.00646	-0.00382	-0.00753
-0.00941	-0.00287	-0.00687
-0.00613	-0.00136	-0.00692
-0.00389	-0.00415	-0.0082
-0.00646	-0.00382	-0.00753

Figure 31. Excel Spreadsheet Humbird.xls

Here we see that the wings start at about $z=\pm0.01$ so that we can *flap* the wings by applying an increasing adjustment in y for z beyond this value. Each triangular element is drawn from the 3 nodes from the list along with the color for this particular element. In order to get the coloring, we must create an outward normal vector, which will change as the wings flap so that these must be recalculated at each step:

```
glBegin(GL_TRIANGLES);
s=2.5*sin(flap*M_PI/180.)-2.;
for(e=0;e<elems;e++)
    {
    i=Elem[e].i;
    j=Elem[e].j;
    k=Elem[e].k;
```

46

```
n1=Node[i];
n2=Node[j];
n3=Node[k];
if(fabs(n1.z)>0.01)
   n1.y+=0.375*(fabs(n1.z)-0.01)*s;
if(fabs(n2.z)>0.01)
   n2.y+=0.375*(fabs(n2.z)-0.01)*s;
if(fabs(n3.z)>0.01)
   n3.y+=0.375*(fabs(n3.z)-0.01)*s;
glColor(Elem[e].rgb);
P.x=(float)(n2.x-n1.x);
P.y=(float)(n2.y-n1.y);
P.z=(float)(n2.z-n1.z);
Q.x=(float)(n3.x-n1.x);
Q.y=(float)(n3.y-n1.y);
Q.z=(float)(n3.z-n1.z);
N=Normalize(CrossProduct(P,Q));
x1=(float)n1.x;
y1=(float)n1.y;
z1=(float)n1.z;
x2=(float)n2.x;
y2=(float)n2.y;
z2=(float)n2.z;
x3=(float)n3.x;
y3=(float)n3.y;
z3=(float)n3.z;
glNormal3f(N.x,N.y,N.z);
glVertex3f(x1,y1,z1);
glVertex3f(x2,y2,z2);
glVertex3f(x3,y3,z3);
}
glEnd();
```
We will apply a more complex *flapping* and also *flex* the wings in the next chapter. For now, we will only consider rigid *flapping*. Note the somewhat bulky mixture of double and single precision floating-point numbers. This is unavoidable, for C presumes all floating-point numbers and constants to be doubles unless typed otherwise with a trailing F or (float) casting, while OpenGL assumes most floating-point numbers are single precision. This is a historical artifact because OpenGL was developed before Intel processors and the Windows operating system became ubiquitous. Speed and storage were much greater concerns in the early days of OpenGL. Intel FPUs (floating-point processing units) often process double precision reals faster than single precision ones and have an 80-bit native format. This was not true for other processors, especially those not having an FPU. I personally recall those days quite clearly and am glad to have left them behind. Three frames of the end result are shown in this next figure:

Figure 32. Rigid Wing Motion

Chapter 6. Flexed Wing Articulation

For this next step we will use a condor. As the hummingbird was fairly stubby, the wing stretching was not particularly noticeable. If we were to use the same formula with the condor, this would look unnatural. Therefore, we will bend (flex) the wings without stretching them. All of the associated files can be found in the examples\condor folder. The GUI is shown below:

Figure 33. Condor Windows GUI

There were only 952 nodes and 1900 triangular elements in the humming bird model. The condor model consists of 5795 nodes and 11,664 elements. These are read in as before. The elements can also be viewed in the Excel spreadsheet condor.xls, which is shown on the next page. The wings extend outward from about z>±0.05 and the tail, which we also want to flex, extends back from about x<-0.15. We can rigidly flap the tail with a simple motion, but the wings will be a little more complicated. We will not consider individual feathers until the next chapter.

Realistic wing flexing may be approximated by the deflection of a cantilever beam with distributed loading. The force of air is distributed over the wing, the wing is attached at the body, plus the bones are thicker toward the body and thinner toward the tips. Structural mechanics is beyond the scope of this text and so the reader is referred to the Web, where many resources, figures, and equations may be found. Such a beam is illustrated in this next figure:

49

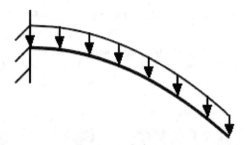

Figure 34. Uniformly Loaded Cantilever Beam

The deflection along any point, x, along the span of a uniformly loaded cantilever beam is given by the following expression:

$$\delta = \frac{wx^2}{24EI}\left(6L^2 - 4Lx + x^2\right)$$ (6.1)

where w is the loading (force per unit length), L is the length of the beam, E is the modulus of elasticity, and I is the area moment of inertia of the cross-section. The particulars are not important for our purposes, but we will utilize the parabolic shape: y=a+bx+cx².

In order to compensate for the stretching effect, we must calculate the arc length along the flexed wing. The calculus of arc lengths is also beyond the scope of this book. Length along an arc or curve is given by the following expression:

$$s = \int_p^q \sqrt{1+\left(\frac{dy}{dx}\right)^2}\, dx$$ (6.2)

For our parabola dy/dx=b+2cx so that:

$$s = \int_p^q \sqrt{1+\left(b+2cx\right)^2}\, dx$$ (6.3)

This expression can be analytically integrated to yield:

$$s = \frac{2\alpha cq + \alpha b + \gamma - 2\beta cp - \beta b - \ln 2 - \ln\left(2cp+b+\beta\right)}{4c}$$ (6.4)

$$\alpha = \sqrt{1+b^2 + 4bcq + 4c^2q^2}$$ (6.5)

$$\beta = \sqrt{1+b^2 + 4bcq + 4c^2p^2}$$ (6.6)

$$\gamma = \ln\left(4cq + 2b + 2r\right)$$ (6.7)

50

Calculation of the arc length along a curve is illustrated in the Excel spreadsheet arc_length_calculus.xls in the equations folder of the online archive. A typical curve and associated calculations are shown below:

Arc Length Calculus
typical curve

discrete		smooth			
x	y	x	y	dy/dx	s
0	76	0	76	-0.40	0
30	60	5	74	-0.45	5
60	39	10	72	-0.50	11
90	32	15	69	-0.50	17
120	64	20	67	-0.58	22
150	123	25	63	-0.68	28
180	165	30	60	-0.70	34
210	137	35	56	-0.70	40
240	52	40	53	-0.70	46
270	0	45	49	-0.70	53
300	60	50	46	-0.70	59

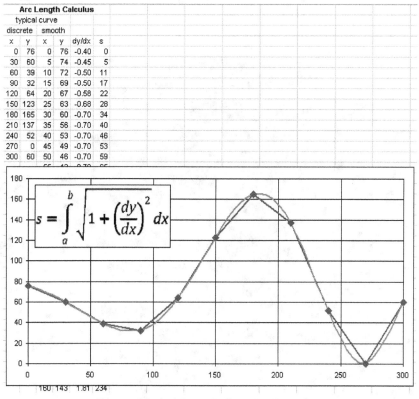

$$s = \int_a^b \sqrt{1 + \left(\frac{dy}{dx}\right)^2}\, dx$$

Figure 35. Arc Length Calculus Example

As the centerline of the condor model lies along y=z=0, the wing length plus body radius is effectively equal to:

$$L_W = \sqrt{y^2 + z^2} \tag{6.8}$$

We can, therefore, simply adjust both coordinates (y and z) of each wing node by the ratio of the length before and after adjustment using the hypot() math function:

```
if(fabs(n1.z)>0.05&&n1.x>-0.155)
  {
  a=hypot(n1.y,n1.z);
  dz=fabs(n1.z)-0.05;
  b=0.375*(9.*s-3.);
  c=b/2.;
```

51

```
dy=(b+c*dz)*dz;
n1.y+=dy;
r=hypot(n1.y,n1.z);
n1.y*=a/r;
n1.z*=a/r;
}
```
The end result is shown in this next figure:

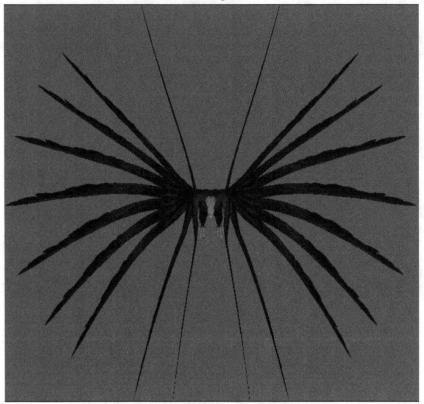

Figure 36. Flexed Wing Articulation

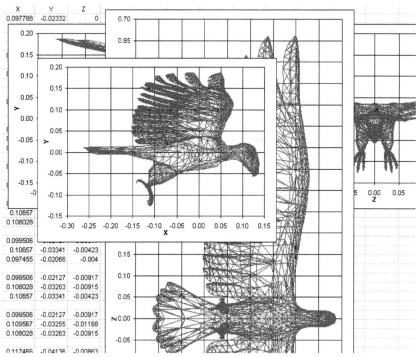

Figure 37. Condor Excel Spreadsheet

53

Chapter 7. Undulating Articulation

Before we get into finer objects such as hair, we will consider waving motion that is more complex than the basically one-dimensional wing flapping. To introduce this next topic, we begin with the TWAVE demo from the original OpenGL SDK. The associated files can be found on the Web. A cleaned-up version is provided in the examples\twave folder. This code eliminates superfluous items, uses standard variable types, and specifically targets the Windows operating system. It can also be compiled without error using Visual Studio, which is a requirement for all of the code discussed in this text. The result is:

Figure 38. TWAVE OpenGL Demo

There are several waving flag demos available on the Web. Another is provided here in the examples\flag folder, which is built upon the program structure of the hummingbird and condor examples with elements from the TWAVE demo.

The Windows GUI deploying the simplest undulation in the y and z directions is shown in this next figure:

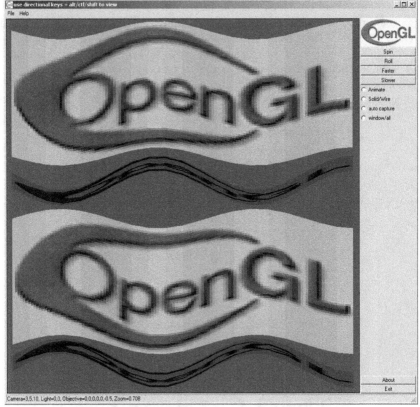

Figure 39. Simplest Flag Undulation

We also incorporate a texture (the OpenGL flag) in this example (also see Appendix B for more on textures). In order to achieve a more natural coloration of filaments (such as hair or fur), we will need to apply a texture.

Chapter 8. Modeling Hair

On our path to create realistic hair or fur, we begin with a few discrete hairs. The general effect we're reaching for is illustrated in this first figure:

Figure 40. Conceptualized Discrete Hairs

Actual individual hairs look like this:

Figure 41. Individual Hair

Our model hairs will be elongated cones, which may bend along the centerline. A curved, shrinking ring of quadrangles (i.e., a *tube*) will form each hair. These are generated in the same way that the cylindrical flagpole and spherical knob were added to the example in the preceding chapter. The x and y location along with the radius are provided as a array. The number of sections along each tube is determined by the number of xyr triads. The code is listed below:

```
#define X(i) XYR[3*(i)]
#define Y(i) XYR[3*(i)+1]
#define R(i) XYR[3*(i)+2]
void RenderTube(double*XYR,int L,int M)
  {
  int i,j,l,m;
  double A,B,*cosA,*cosB,Rm,Rx,*sinA,*sinB,Xm,Xx,Ym,Yx;
  VECTOR*N,*V;
  if(L<3)
    return;
  if(M<3)
    return;
  Rm=Rx=R(0);
  Xm=Xx=X(0);
  Ym=Yx=Y(0);
  for(l=1;l<L;l++)
    {
    if(R(l)<Rm)
      Rm=R(l);
    if(R(l)>Rx)
      Rx=R(l);
    if(X(l)<Xm)
      Xm=X(l);
    if(X(l)>Xx)
      Xx=X(l);
    if(Y(l)<Ym)
      Ym=Y(l);
    if(Y(l)>Yx)
      Yx=Y(l);
    }
  if(Rm>=Rx)
    return;
  if(Xm>=Xx)
    return;
  if(Ym>=Yx)
    return;
  cosA=calloc(L,sizeof(double));
  sinA=calloc(L,sizeof(double));
  for(l=0;l<L;l++)
    {
    i=max(0,l-1);
    j=min(L-1,l+1);
    A=atan2(X(i)-X(j),Y(j)-Y(i));
    cosA[l]=cos(A);
    sinA[l]=sin(A);
    }
  cosB=calloc(M,sizeof(double));
```

```
sinB=calloc(M,sizeof(double));
for(m=0;m<M;m++)
    {
    B=m*2.*M_PI/M;
    cosB[m]=cos(B);
    sinB[m]=sin(B);
    }
N=calloc(L*M,sizeof(VECTOR));
V=calloc(L*M,sizeof(VECTOR));
for(i=l=0;l<L;l++)
    {
    for(m=0;m<M;m++,i++)
        {
        N[i].x=(float)(cosB[m]*cosA[l]);
        N[i].y=(float)(cosB[m]*sinA[l]);
        N[i].z=(float)(sinB[m]);
        V[i].x=(float)(X(l)+R(l)*N[i].x);
        V[i].y=(float)(Y(l)+R(l)*N[i].y);
        V[i].z=(float)(     R(l)*N[i].z);
        }
    }
for(l=0;l<L-1;l++)
    {
    glBegin(GL_QUAD_STRIP);
    for(m=0;m<=M;m++)
        {
        i=M*l+m%M;
        j=M*(l+1)+m%M;
        glNormal3d(N[i].x,N[i].y,N[i].z);
        glVertex3d(V[i].x,V[i].y,V[i].z);
        glNormal3d(N[j].x,N[j].y,N[j].z);
        glVertex3d(V[j].x,V[j].y,V[j].z);
        }
    glEnd();
    }
free(V);
free(N);
free(cosA);
free(sinA);
free(cosB);
free(sinB);
}
#undef R
#undef Y
#undef X
```

We begin with 400 brown hairs evenly spaced over a pink patch of appropriate size with a light blue background. The *scalp* has a slight curvature and extends slightly beyond the hairs. The files can be found in folder examples\hair.

59

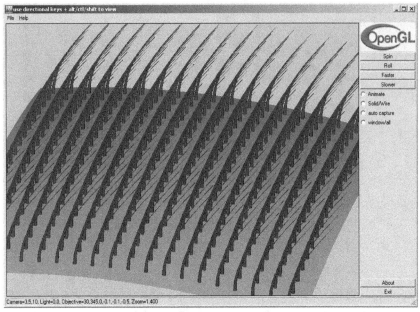

Figure 42. 100 Approximate Hairs

Next, we need a minimal head model with scalp elements identified.

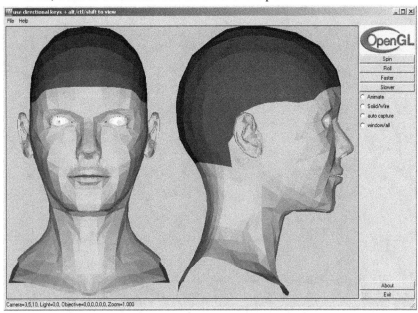

Figure 43. Minimal Head Model

This generic woman and also a generic man head can be found in the models folder of the online archive. We now want to attach one or more hairs to each of the triangular scalp elements. This is what one hair per element sticking upward looks like:

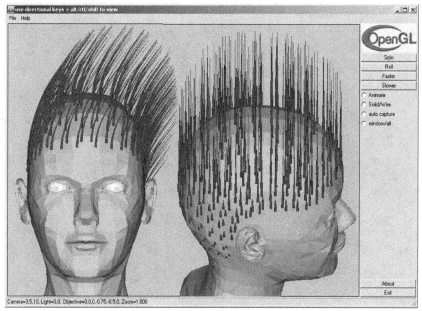

Figure 44. Without Localized Direction

Getting the direction (and eventually curvature) of the hairs will take more effort, as we shall see. Rendering spiked hair is quite simple,

```
void RenderHair(double u,double v,double w,double
    s,double x,double y,double z)
{
glLineWidth(5.F);
glBegin(GL_LINES);
glVertex3d(x,y,z);
glVertex3d((float)(x+0.5*s*u),(float)(y+0.5*s*v),
    (float)(z+0.5*s*w));
glEnd();
}
```

We are already calculating the outward normals, as these must be used for lighting. This gives us the initial direction of the hairs. We can use these to render spiked hairs sticking out in all directions, as shown in this next figure:

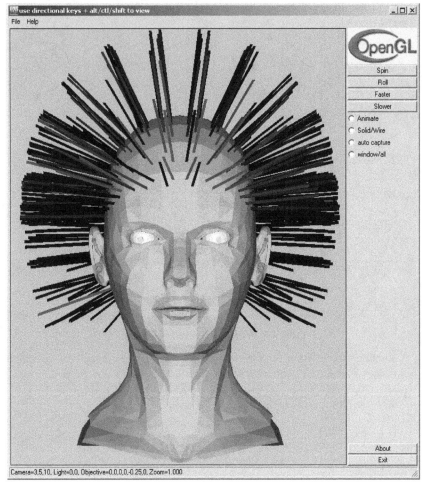

Figure 45. Spiked Tubular Hair

We can add an downward (or upward) gravity-like effect by arcing toward -y (down or +y up) proportional to the distance along the hair, s².

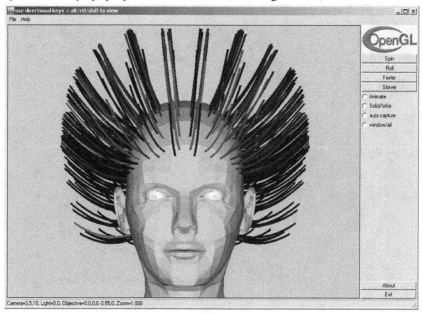

Figure 46. Spike Hair with Upward Sweep

We ultimately want to draw tapered tubes rather than simple lines (see Figures 42 and 44). Not only would these provide proper lighting effects but also textures. Rotation of each hair using calls to glRotatesf() so as to obtain the proper curvature is more problematic than it might seem. It is more effective to extrude each hair along a curved path line, as with the teapot spout and handle.

Figure 47. Classic OpenGL Teapot

63

Details of the tapered tubular hairs are shown in this next figure:

Figure 48. Tubular Hair Detail

The math we need is the same as the 3D coil demo built into TP2:

Figure 49. 3D Coil

Each ring in the coil lies in a plane perpendicular to the centerline. More specifically, these planes are defined by two orthogonal vectors, **u** and **v**. The cross product of these two vectors (**u**×**v**=**s**) lies along the centerline of the coil. If **s** is the parametric centerline and t is the distance along the centerline, then the vector **s** is given by:

$$\vec{s} = \begin{array}{c} \dfrac{dx}{dt}\,\hat{i} \\[2mm] \dfrac{dy}{dt}\,\hat{j} \\[2mm] \dfrac{dz}{dt}\,\hat{k} \end{array} \qquad (8.1)$$

If the vectors **u** and **v** are normalized and φ is the angle around the centerline, then a circle of radius r in the perpendicular plane at the point (x,y,z) is given by:

$$\begin{array}{c} x + r\left(u_x \cos\varphi + v_y \sin\varphi\right)\hat{i} \\[2mm] y + r\left(u_y \cos\varphi + v_y \sin\varphi\right)\hat{j} \\[2mm] z + r\left(u_z \cos\varphi + v_z \sin\varphi\right)\hat{k} \end{array} \qquad (8.2)$$

The angle in the xy plane, θ, is given by:

$$\tan\theta = -\frac{\left(\dfrac{dx}{dt}\right)}{\left(\dfrac{dy}{dt}\right)} \qquad (8.3)$$

If we require **u** to be in the xy plane, we have:

$$\begin{aligned} u_x &= \sin\theta \\ u_y &= \cos\theta \\ u_z &= 0 \end{aligned} \qquad (8.4)$$

As **u** and **v** are perpendicular, their dot product is equal to zero:

$$u_x v_x + u_y v_y + u_z v_z = 0 \qquad (8.5)$$

Combining these relationships yields the second vector, **v**:

$$v_x = -\frac{dz}{dt}\cos\theta$$

$$v_y = \frac{dz}{dt}\sin\theta \qquad (8.6)$$

$$v_z = \begin{cases} \dfrac{dx}{dt}\dfrac{1}{\cos\theta} \\ \dfrac{dy}{dt}\dfrac{-1}{\sin\theta} \end{cases}$$

With these equations, we can now draw a tapering *tube* beginning at a given point arbitrarily meandering in three dimensions. There is also a small program (coil.c) in the models folder that creates a single tube and illustrates the mathematics in a minimal context. The complex *tube* is rendered with the following code that first calculates the position of all the nodes, then rolls them out as quad strips for each section along the centerline. The outward normals are calculated for each section of the quad strip as it's being added.

```
typedef struct{float r,t,x,y,z;}RTXYZ;
void RenderComplexTube(RTXYZ*rtxyz,int n,int m)
  {
  int i,i1,i2,i3,j,k;
  float a,c,dxdt,dydt,dzdt,phi,s,theta;
  VECTOR p,u,v,*w;
  w=calloc(n*m,sizeof(VECTOR));
  for(k=i=0;i<n;i++)
    {
    if(i==0)
      {
      i1=i;
      i2=i+1;
      }
    else if(i==n-1)
      {
      i1=n-2;
      i2=n-1;
      }
    else
      {
      i1=i-1;
      i2=i+1;
      }
    dxdt=(rtxyz[i2].x-rtxyz[i1].x)/
      (rtxyz[i2].t-rtxyz[i1].t);
    dydt=(rtxyz[i2].y-rtxyz[i1].y)/
      (rtxyz[i2].t-rtxyz[i1].t);
    dzdt=(rtxyz[i2].z-rtxyz[i1].z)/
```

```
            (rtxyz[i2].t-rtxyz[i1].t);
        theta=(float)(-atan2(dydt,dxdt));
        phi=(float)atan2(hypot(dxdt,dydt),dzdt);
        u.x=(float)sin(theta);
        u.y=(float)cos(theta);
        u.z=0.F;
        if(fabs(cos(theta))>fabs(sin(theta)))
            v.z=(float)(dxdt/cos(theta));
        else
            v.z=(float)(-dydt/sin(theta));
        v.x=(float)(-dzdt*cos(theta));
        v.y=(float)(dzdt*sin(theta));
        a=(float)sqrt(v.x*v.x+v.y*v.y+v.z*v.z);
        v.x/=a;
        v.y/=a;
        v.z/=a;
        for(j=0;j<m;j++,k++)
        {
            c=(float)cos(j*2.*M_PI/m);
            s=(float)sin(j*2.*M_PI/m);
            w[k].x=(float)(rtxyz[i].x
                +rtxyz[i].r*(s*u.x+c*v.x));
            w[k].y=(float)(rtxyz[i].y
                +rtxyz[i].r*(s*u.y+c*v.y));
            w[k].z=(float)(rtxyz[i].z
                +rtxyz[i].r*(s*u.z+c*v.z));
        }
    }
    for(i=0;i<n-1;i++)
    {
        glBegin(GL_QUAD_STRIP);
        for(j=0;j<=m;j++)
        {
            i1=m*i+(j%m);
            i2=m*(i+1)+(j%m);
            i3=m*(i+1)+((j+1)%m);
            u.x=w[i2].x-w[i1].x;
            u.y=w[i2].y-w[i1].y;
            u.z=w[i2].z-w[i1].z;
            v.x=w[i3].x-w[i1].x;
            v.y=w[i3].y-w[i1].y;
            v.z=w[i3].z-w[i1].z;
            p=Normalize(CrossProduct(u,v));
            glNormal3d(p.x,p.y,p.z);
            glVertex3f(w[i1].x,w[i1].y,w[i1].z);
            glVertex3f(w[i2].x,w[i2].y,w[i2].z);
        }
        glEnd();
    }
```

```
    free(w);
    }
```

The end result is shown in this next figure, which has the hair shape from Figure 44 and the curvature from Figure 46:

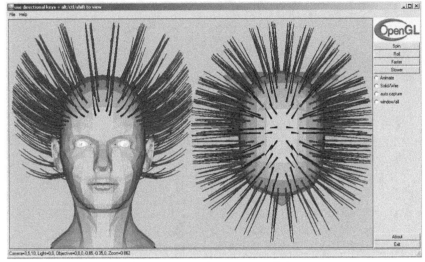

Figure 50. Complex Tube Hairs

The complex hair is then reduced to the following brief code:

```
void RenderComplexHair(double u,double v,double w,double
    s,double x,double y,double z)
    {
    int i,n;
    double g,l,r;
    RTXYZ rtxyz[11];
    l=0.5*s;
    g=hypot(u,w)*l/2.;
    n=sizeof(rtxyz)/sizeof(RTXYZ);
    r=0.01;
    for(i=0;i<n;i++)
        {
        rtxyz[i].t=(float)(i/(n-1.));
        rtxyz[i].r=(float)(r);
        rtxyz[i].x=(float)(x+i*u*l/(n-1));
        rtxyz[i].y=(float)(y+i*v*l/(n-1)+i*i*g/(n-1)/(n-1));
        rtxyz[i].z=(float)(z+i*w*l/(n-1));
        r*=0.9;
        }
    RenderComplexTube(rtxyz,n,16);
    }
```

The next step toward realism is adding more thinner hairs. We first increase from one to three per scalp element and divide the diameter by two. The end result, which is starting to look a little more reasonable, is shown below:

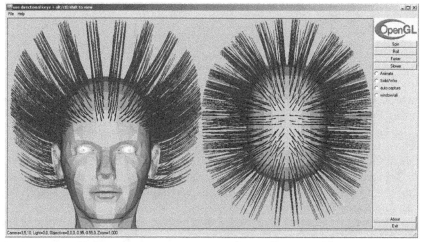

Figure 51. Three Complex Tube Hairs per Element

Next 7 hairs and one-fourth the diameter…

Figure 52. Seven Complex Tube Hairs per Element

These would be more realistic were they somewhat randomly spaced. We will eventually get there after considering various motions and color effects. At this level of detail, the rendering time is from one to two seconds, depending on the processor. While real-time animation has been practical up until this point with the other examples, it is not practical at this level of detail. That is why we

69

have built in the capability of *auto capture* to store sequential frames as individual files that can be combined to create an animated GIF.

The number of hairs per elements should be proportional to the area. The area of a triangle in 3D is given by Heron's formula:

$$a = \sqrt{s(s-a)(s-b)(s-c)}$$
$$s = \frac{a+b+c}{2} \tag{8.7}$$

where a, b, c are the lengths of the three sides. The side lengths are calculated using the Pythagorean theorem. The average area per scalp element is 0.00643. The largest is 0.01541, about 2.4 times the average. The smallest is 0.00178, about 0.28 times the average. Evenly spacing our previous density would be about 2 hairs in the smallest element and 17 in the largest or about one hair per 0.001 area unit. Increasing from an average of 7 to 21, spacing these randomly and proportional to element area, yields a slightly better result but also triples the time to render.

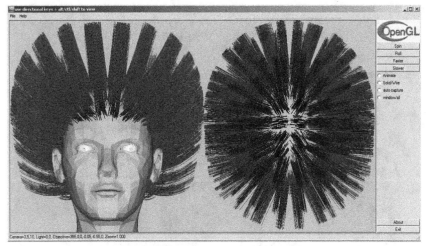

Figure 53. Twenty-One Randomly Spaced Hairs per Element

We are approaching a minimal acceptable density. We can still see clumping. Adding a random x and z component to the gravity term will diminish this effect. This next figure shows the addition of random x and y.

70

Figure 54.Twenty-One Randomly Spaced Hairs with Random XY

We still need at least three times greater density and also random lengths. With this step we achieve a somewhat realistic frizz.

Figure 55. Sixty-Three Average Hairs per Element with Random XYL

The rendering time is now six to twelve seconds and so we now introduce delayed painting. This was covered in the two previous texts in this series. Basically, we draw some of the elements and set a flag. We also add another timer. When this timer is called, if the current rendering is complete and the flag is set, then all of the elements are redrawn and the flag is reset.

The temporary rendering pending a full repaint is shown in this next figure:

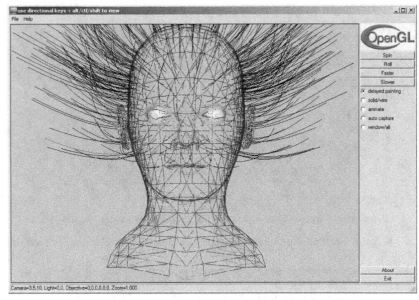

Figure 56. Partial Rendering with Pending Repaint

We next want to replace the frizz with down swept hair. This means the top hairs must be displaced laterally (in ±x) and into the screen (-z) so that they don't fall back into the head. We also want to deploy normal gravity (-y).

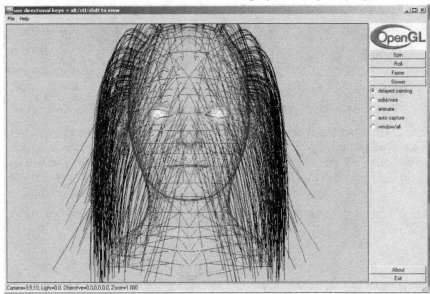

Figure 57. Partial Rendering with Downward Gravity

While this next full rendering won't make the cover of *Vogue*, it is a reasonable approximation of hair.

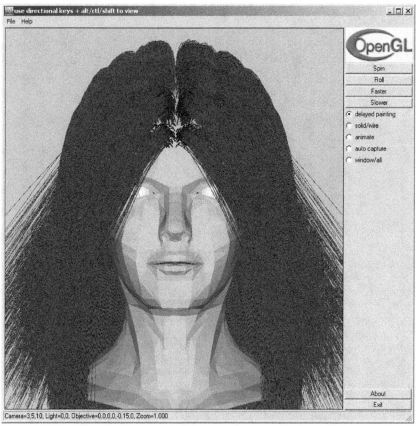

Figure 58. First Reasonable Approximation

The hairs must randomly *jittered* along the part to make it less pronounced. This can be accomplished by adding small random adjustments to each component of the normal vector.

```
if(hypot(x,z)<0.1)
  {
  u+=xrand()/10.;
  v+=xrand()/10.;
  w+=xrand()/10.;
  }
```

Another way to control the path of the hairs from the scalp out would be to define a *hoop* and use this as a sort of *target*. Such a hoop is shown in the next two figures.

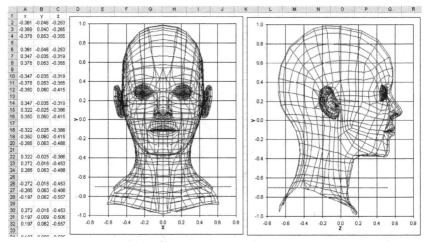

	x	y	z
2	-0.361	-0.046	-0.253
3	-0.389	0.040	-0.265
4	-0.378	0.053	-0.355
5			
6	0.361	-0.046	-0.253
7	0.347	-0.035	-0.319
8	0.378	0.053	-0.355
9			
10	-0.347	-0.035	-0.319
11	-0.378	0.053	-0.355
12	-0.350	0.060	-0.415
13			
14	0.347	-0.035	-0.319
15	0.322	-0.025	-0.386
16	0.350	0.060	-0.415
17			
18	-0.322	-0.025	-0.386
19	-0.350	0.060	-0.415
20	-0.285	0.063	-0.488
21			
22	0.322	-0.025	-0.386
23	0.272	-0.016	-0.453
24	0.285	0.063	-0.488
25			
26	-0.272	-0.016	-0.453
27	-0.285	0.063	-0.488
28	-0.197	0.062	-0.557
29			
30	0.272	-0.016	-0.453
31	0.197	-0.009	-0.505
32	0.197	0.062	-0.557
33			

Figure 59. Vertical Position of Hoop

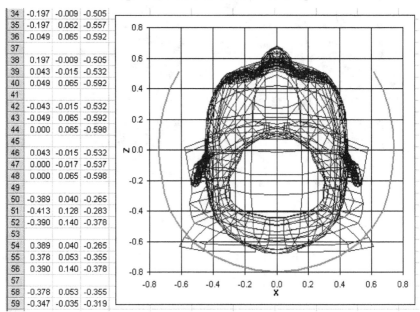

34	-0.197	-0.009	-0.505
35	-0.197	0.062	-0.557
36	-0.049	0.065	-0.592
37			
38	0.197	-0.009	-0.505
39	0.043	-0.015	-0.532
40	0.049	0.065	-0.592
41			
42	-0.043	-0.015	-0.532
43	-0.049	0.065	-0.592
44	0.000	0.065	-0.598
45			
46	0.043	-0.015	-0.532
47	0.000	-0.017	-0.537
48	0.000	0.065	-0.598
49			
50	-0.389	0.040	-0.265
51	-0.413	0.128	-0.283
52	-0.390	0.140	-0.378
53			
54	0.389	0.040	-0.265
55	0.378	0.053	-0.355
56	0.390	0.140	-0.378
57			
58	-0.378	0.053	-0.355
59	-0.347	-0.035	-0.319

Figure 60. Hoop in the X-Z Plane

We can pick the closest point on the hoop and bend the hair toward it. To add realism, we can also jitter the destination in xyz.

```
if(style_option==2)
    {
    for(j=i=0;i<m;i++)
        {
```

74

```
rr=hypot3d(x-hoop[i].x,y-hoop[i].y,z-hoop[i].z);
if(i==0)
    rm=rr;
else if(rr<rm)
    {
    rm=rr;
    j=i;
    }
}
if(j>0)
    i=j-1;
else
    i=1;
q=drand();
h.x=(float)(q*hoop[i].x+(1.-q)*hoop[j].x);
h.y=(float)(q*hoop[i].y+(1.-q)*hoop[j].y);
h.z=(float)(q*hoop[i].z+(1.-q)*hoop[j].z);
h.x+=(float)(xrand()/50.);
h.y+=(float)(xrand()/50.);
h.z+=(float)(xrand()/50.);
```
The piecewise approximation of this path is calculated linearly:
```
for(i=0;i<n;i++)
    {
    t=i/(n-1.);
    rtxyz[i].t=(float)t;
    rtxyz[i].r=(float)r;
    if(i<n/2)
        {
        rtxyz[i].x=(float)(x+i*u*l/(n-1));
        rtxyz[i].y=(float)(y+i*v*l/(n-1));
        rtxyz[i].z=(float)(z+i*w*l/(n-1));
        }
    else
        {
        q=(n-1-i)*2./n;
        rtxyz[i].x=(float)(q*rtxyz[n/2-1].x+(1.-q)*h.x);
        rtxyz[i].y=(float)(q*rtxyz[n/2-1].y+(1.-q)*h.y);
        rtxyz[i].z=(float)(q*rtxyz[n/2-1].z+(1.-q)*h.z);
        }
    r*=0.9;
    }
```
To spread the bangs away from the eyes, we add:
```
for(i=1;i<n;i++)
    if(rtxyz[i].z>=0.4)
        if(rtxyz[i].y<=0.45)
            if(fabs(rtxyz[i].x)<0.5)
                rtxyz[i].x=(float)sign(0.5,rtxyz[i].x);
```

This leaves a jointed unrealistic path between two points, starting perpendicular to the scalp element and ending near the hoop. In order to achieve a smooth curve, we add some level of smoothing, in this case 3 passes.

```
for(j=0;j<3;j++)
  {
  for(i=1;i<n-1;i++)
    {
    rtxyz[i].x=(rtxyz[i-1].x+rtxyz[i+1].x)/2.F;
    rtxyz[i].y=(rtxyz[i-1].y+rtxyz[i+1].y)/2.F;
    rtxyz[i].z=(rtxyz[i-1].z+rtxyz[i+1].z)/2.F;
    }
  }
```

When pre-drawing (delayed painting enabled), we use line segments. When making the final pass, we draw the complex tubes.

```
if(partial_paint)
  {
  glBegin(GL_LINE_STRIP);
  for(i=0;i<n;i++)
    glVertex3d(rtxyz[i].x,rtxyz[i].y,rtxyz[i].z);
  glEnd();
  }
else
  RenderComplexTube(rtxyz,n,16);
```

These various options are selected by parameters at the top of the code:

```
#define thick_lines      1
#define simple_tubes     2
#define complex_tubes    3
#define rendering        3
int downswept_hairs   = 1;
int hairs_per_element=63;
int randomize_gravity= 1;
int randomize_lengths= 1;
int style_option      = 2;
```

We can also change the colors, for instance of the pupils.

```
  else
  if(style_option==1&&(Elem[e].rgb==pink||Elem[e].rgb==
  green))
    glColor(brown);
  else if(style_option==2&&Elem[e].rgb==pink)
    glColor(0xFFDFBF);
  else if(style_option==2&&Elem[e].rgb==green)
    glColor(blue);
  else
    glColor(Elem[e].rgb);
```

76

The end result for Style Option 1 is shown in this next figure:

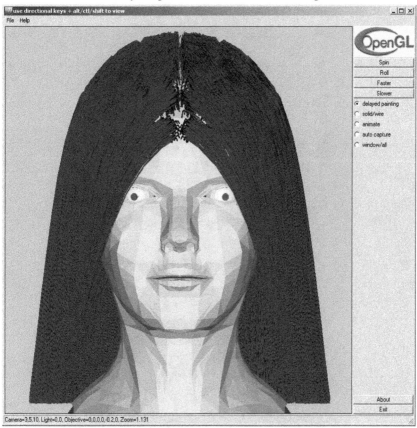

Figure 61. Style Option 1 with Hoop and Parted Bangs

We can change a few parameters to produce a different appearance, changing the skin tone and pupil coloration:

```
if(Elem[e].rgb==brown)
  {
  if(style_option==1)
    glColor(black);
  else if(style_option==2)
    glColor(dark_red);
  else
    glColor(brown);
```

This combination is Style Option 2:

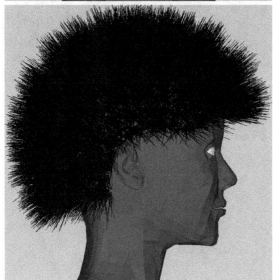

Figure 62. Style Option 2

Appendix A. Working with Pixel Contexts

The term *pixel context* is tossed about in OpenGL literature as if it were intuitive or had meaning in a broad context. It doesn't, particularly in the context of Windows programming. The Windows APIs use completely different terminology and the documentation doesn't mention pixel contexts. While the terminology is unfamiliar, the concepts are not.

In order to paint anything in Windows you must have a handle to a *device context*. When this device context is in memory, it's called a *compatible* device context. In order to paint on the display without flicker, you must first build the image in memory and then BitBlt it onto the display. Color images in memory are called DIB sections in Windows. You must select the DIB section into the memory device context. The combination of a memory device context and a DIB section (plus a few other things, including a Z-buffer) is called a pixel context.

OpenGL only works with pixel contexts. You can see what pixel contexts are available by calling DescribePixelFormat(). You select the one you want by calling SetPixelFormat(). You prepare it for use with OpenGL by calling wglCreateContext() and distinguishing this one context from many by calling wglMakeCurrent(). When it comes time to paint it onto the display, you call SwapBuffers(), which just *paints* them rather than actually *swapping* them.

Pixel contexts, along with these virtually undocumented Windows API calls, are defined in wingdi.h and ntgdi.h. Other than facilitating OpenGL rendering, it's not clear why these even exist in the Windows context or why they are linked in gdi32.lib and implemented in gdi32.dll. Whatever the reason, this is what they are and you must utilize them to do anything with OpenGL.

You must first get a pixel context before doing anything with OpenGL. You don't get to *request* (or *specify*) a particular pixel context; rather, you must *select* one from a list that will work for you intend to do. You get a list of available formats by calling DescribePixelFormat(). The following is a typical list of such formats:

index	OpenGL	double buffer	RGBA	need palette	system palette	color bits	depth bits	stencil bits	generic	accele- rated	score	stencil score
1	1	0	1	0	0	32	24	0	0	0	0	0
2	1	0	1	0	0	32	24	0	0	0	0	0
3	1	0	1	0	0	32	24	8	0	1	0	0
4	1	0	1	0	0	32	24	8	0	0	0	0
5	1	0	1	0	0	32	0	0	0	0	0	0
6	1	0	1	0	0	32	0	0	0	0	0	0
7	1	1	1	0	0	32	24	0	0	0	80	0
8	1	1	1	0	0	32	24	0	0	0	80	0
9	1	1	1	0	0	32	24	8	0	1	88	88
10	1	1	1	0	0	32	24	8	0	0	80	80
11	1	1	1	0	0	32	0	0	0	0	64	0
12	1	1	1	0	0	32	0	0	0	0	64	0
13	1	1	1	0	0	32	24	0	0	0	80	0
14	1	1	1	0	0	32	24	0	0	0	80	0
19	0	1	1	0	0	32	24	0	0	0	0	0
90	0	1	1	0	0	32	24	8	0	0	0	0
91	1	0	1	0	0	32	32	8	1	1	0	0
92	1	0	1	0	0	32	16	8	1	0	0	0
93	1	1	1	0	0	32	32	8	1	1	90	90
94	1	1	1	0	0	32	16	8	1	0	82	82
95	1	0	1	0	0	32	32	8	1	1	0	0
96	1	0	1	0	0	32	16	8	1	0	0	0
97	1	1	1	0	0	32	32	8	1	0	82	82
98	1	1	1	0	0	32	16	8	1	0	82	82
99	1	0	0	0	0	32	32	8	1	1	0	0
100	1	0	0	0	0	32	16	8	1	0	0	0
101	1	1	0	0	0	32	32	8	1	1	0	0
102	1	1	0	0	0	32	16	8	1	0	0	0
105	1	0	1	0	0	24	32	8	1	0	0	0
106	1	0	1	0	0	24	16	8	1	0	0	0
107	1	0	0	0	0	24	32	8	1	0	0	0
108	1	0	0	0	0	24	16	8	1	0	0	0
111	1	0	1	0	0	16	32	8	1	0	0	0
112	1	0	1	0	0	16	16	8	1	0	0	0
113	1	0	0	0	0	16	32	8	1	0	0	0
114	1	0	0	0	0	16	16	8	1	0	0	0
125	1	0	0	1	1	4	32	8	1	0	0	0
126	1	0	0	1	1	4	16	8	1	0	0	0

This table has been abbreviated for space, but still illustrates the process you must go through in order to select an appropriate pixel context. First of all, some of the available formats don't even support OpenGL. These are eliminated immediately. Ones that don't support double buffering or require a palette can also be eliminated. OpenGL depends on RGBA, so formats that don't support this can also be eliminated. The color depth should be at least 24 and will paint faster if this matches the depth of the display device context.

The depth bits are used for the Z-buffer and must be at least 16. Generic doesn't matter. Accelerated may draw faster, but is not always available, depending on hardware and drivers. If you want to use stenciling, that can be included in the criteria. I calculate a score for each and pick the one with the highest score. If none of the available formats score above zero, exit the program. The following code snippet implements this selection process:

```
HDC GetBestPixelFormat(HDC hDC,int stencil)
{
int i,j,n,s,sx;
PIXELFORMATDESCRIPTOR pfd;
if((n=DescribePixelFormat(hDC,1,0,NULL))<1)
return(NULL);
j=sx=-1;
for(i=1;i<=n;i++)
{
DescribePixelFormat(hDC,i,
   sizeof(PIXELFORMATDESCRIPTOR),&pfd);
if(!(pfd.dwFlags&PFD_SUPPORT_OPENGL))
 continue;
if(!(pfd.dwFlags&PFD_DOUBLEBUFFER))
 continue;
if(pfd.iPixelType!=PFD_TYPE_RGBA)
 continue;
if(pfd.dwFlags&PFD_NEED_PALETTE)
 continue;
if(pfd.dwFlags&PFD_NEED_SYSTEM_PALETTE)
 continue;
if(pfd.cColorBits<24)
 continue;
if(pfd.cDepthBits<16)
 continue;
if((1<<pfd.cStencilBits)<stencil)
 continue;
s=pfd.cDepthBits/16;
if(pfd.dwFlags&PFD_GENERIC_ACCELERATED)
 s+=2;
if(pfd.cColorBits==GetDeviceCaps(hDC,BITSPIXEL))
 s+=8;
else if(pfd.cColorBits>=24)
 s+=4;
```

```
if(s<sx)
 continue;
sx=s;
j=i;
}
if(j<0)
return(NULL);
DescribePixelFormat(hDC,j,
   sizeof(PIXELFORMATDESCRIPTOR),&pfd);
if(!SetPixelFormat(hDC,j,&pfd))
return(NULL);
return(hDC);
}
```

A pixel context must be selected and implemented. This is a three-step process, as illustrated in the following code snippet:

```
if((pDC=GetBestPixelFormat(hPlot))==0)
   Abort(__LINE__,"can't find best pixel context\nerror
   code %i",GetLastError());
if((rDC=wglCreateContext(pDC))==0)
   Abort(__LINE__,"can't create OpenGL context\nerror
   code %i",GetLastError());
if(!wglMakeCurrent(pDC,rDC))
   Abort(__LINE__,"can't make OpenGL context
   current\nerror code %i",GetLastError());
```

You will also need to declare the following variables:

```
HDC pDC;    /* plot window device context */
HGLRC rDC;  /* OpenGL rendering context */
int pFS;    /* pixel format selector */
PIXELFORMATDESCRIPTOR pFd;
```

The rendering process also has several steps:

```
glClearDepth(1);
glClearColor(0,0,0,0);
glClearStencil(0);
glClear(GL_COLOR_BUFFER_BIT|
   GL_DEPTH_BUFFER_BIT|GL_STENCIL_BUFFER_BIT);
insert rendering instructions here
guFinish();
SwapBuffers(pDC);
```

Appendix B. Working with Textures

Textures are 32-bit (DWORD) bitmaps ordered: RGBA. These don't have a header, as is the case with a Windows BITMAP (i.e., BITMAPINFOHEADER structure). Instead, the dimensions are specified in a call to the rendering engine:

```
glTexImage2D(GL_TEXTURE_2D,0,3,bi->biWidth,
   bi->biHeight,0,GL_BGR_EXT,
   GL_UNSIGNED_BYTE,(BYTE*)bits);
```

The RGBA bits are entered by row and in the same order (bottom up) as a Windows BITMAP. The width and height must both be a power of two, though not necessarily the same (i.e., 2, 4, 8, 16, 32, 64, 128, 256, 512, or 1024). Texture bitmaps can be quite large, considering there is no compression. Neither Windows nor OpenGL recognize JPEGs as such. If you want to keep the texture as a JPEG, you must also provide your own code to unpack it. Such a code (jpeg6b.c) can be found in the online archive accompanying this and several other of my texts. The JPEGS can easily be handled as resources and loaded when a program starts up. The following is a typical section of a resource file (*.RC):

```
#undef RT_RCDATA
#define RT_RCDATA 0xA

Agate         RT_RCDATA "agate.jpg"
BlackGranite  RT_RCDATA "blackgranite.jpg"
Lapis         RT_RCDATA "lapis.jpg"
Malachite     RT_RCDATA "malachite.jpg"
Marble        RT_RCDATA "marble.jpg"
Oak           RT_RCDATA "oak.jpg"
Pedauk        RT_RCDATA "pedauk.jpg"
Purpleheart   RT_RCDATA "purpleheart.jpg"
Walnut        RT_RCDATA "walnut.jpg"
WhiteGranite  RT_RCDATA "whitegranite.jpg"
Yew           RT_RCDATA "yew.jpg"
Kewazinga     RT_RCDATA "kewazinga.jpg"
```

Note the redefinition of constant RT_RCDATA, which is used for user-defined unstructured binary objects. Some versions of Visual Studio contain a bug. If you don't redefine this constant in the resource file, you will not be able later to load the resource. The other types (e.g., ICON, BITMAP, DIALOG) appear to work well enough. It is also not necessary to redefine RT_RCDATA in the source code (*.C). Preparation of 24-bit images is a simple reordering (don't forget that Windows bitmaps are aligned on DWORD boundaries, while OpenGL bitmaps aren't).

```
wide=4*((bm->biWidth*24+31)/32);
add=wide-3*bm->biWidth;
for(h=0;h<bm->biHeight;h++)
   {
```

```
for(w=0;w<bm->biWidth;w++)
  {
  r=*bits++;
  g=*bits++;
  b=*bits++;
  *stib++=b;
  *stib++=g;
  *stib++=r;
  }
bits+=add;
}
```

Preparation of palette-based (8 bit or less) bitmaps is straightforward:

```
if(bHead->biBitCount<=8)
  {
  map=allocate(__LINE__,bHead->biWidth*bHead-
>biHeight*3,1);
  pal=((BYTE*)bHead)+sizeof(BITMAPINFOHEADER);
  pix=pal+bHead->biClrUsed*sizeof(DWORD);
  if(bHead->biBitCount==8)
    {
    for(h=i=j=0;h<bHead->biHeight;h++)
      {
      for(w=0;w<bHead->biWidth;w++)
        {
        k=pix[i++];
        map[j++]=pal[4*k];
        map[j++]=pal[4*k+1];
        map[j++]=pal[4*k+2];
        }
      }
    }
```

Appendix C. Format Conversions Using TP2

I developed TPLOT in 1980 while working on my doctorate to graphically display the data I was collecting in the laboratory. It originally only worked on one device: Tektronix 4010. That's where the "T" in TPLOT came from. Over the years I added many devices and continued to use TPLOT as I worked in industry. TPLOT was written in FORTRAN, which became increasingly problematic, as operating systems evolved. In the summer of 1993, I began work on the second generation of TPLOT, which I named TP2. This new code was written in C, which opened up many more devices, but it was still not technically a Windows® application. That change didn't come until the spring of 1998. There have been dozens of revisions and additions since then. TP2 is available free online:

https://dudleybenton.altervista.org/software/index.html

Perhaps the biggest difference between TP2 and similar graphic utilities is file types. For instance, the file extension doesn't mean anything to Tecplot™[1]. That is, the same data could be stored in a file with any extension. For Tecplot™ the data structure is defined by various headers and there can be multiple types of data in the same file. For TP2 the data structure is identified by the file extension, as indicated below, and there can be only one data structure in a file.

filename.extention

In order to control how the data is presented in Tecplot™ you also need a layout file (usually, but not necessarily, filename.lay). TP2 displays data based on the type, which is indicated by the file extension. Tecplot™ will display 3D data as 3D or 2D with or without contours, shading, slicing, etc. TP2 will always display 3D data in 3D, unless you are specifically slicing at a plane. TP2 recognizes many more data structures than Tecplot™ (27 in all), each one having a different file extension. TP2 also has a layout (file extension TP2) and can display data from multiple files and of multiple structures, but this isn't mandatory, as with Tecplot™.

Surfaces and Volumes

Both Tecplot™ and TP2 handle 2D surfaces and 3D volumes. The display is similar, but the data structures are different. Tecplot™ requires the file to contain every x,y,z for 2D or x,y,z,w for 3D. One of the main motivations for developing TP2 was efficiency and compactness, including the smallest possible file sizes. If the surface or volume is complete (i.e., rectangular), whether or not the spacing is uniform, there is a definite pattern so that it is superfluous to enter

---

[1] Tecplot™ is a powerful and versatile tool for visualization of many different types of data, but particularly fluid flow, as this software arose from and was motivated by early CFD research. The developers of this software had connections with NASA and were deeply involved with aerodynamics. This excellent product can be found at their web site: https://www.tecplot.com/

all of the points except for z in 2D and w in 3D. That's how TP2 works. Surfaces are defined by a 2D table (file extension TB2) and volumes are defined by a 3D table (file extension TB3). The data are entered as a list of x's, then y's, then z's, then w's—not each and every x,y,z,w.

Finite Elements

Finite elements (triangles, quadrangles, tetrahedra, bricks, etc.) are very similar in Tecplot™ and TP2. The file structure consists of a list of nodes followed by a list of element indices. For TP2 2D finite elements have a file extension of 2DV and 3D finite elements have the extension 3DV.

Velocity Vectors

Velocity vectors are handled differently. In Tecplot™ the velocity components (typically u, v, and w) can be in any column, but are defined along with spatial coordinates (x, y, and z). With TP2 2D velocity vectors consist of x, y, u, and v—in that order and in a file having the extension V2D. Three-dimensional velocity vectors consist of x, y, z, u, v, and w—in that order and in a file having the extension V3D.

Layout

As mentioned before, Tecplot™ *requires* a layout file, which usually has the extension LAY. TP2 accepts an *optional* layout file, which has the extension TP2. With TP2, you can override any file extension (for example reading 2D velocity vectors from a file with extension VEC) by appending a minus followed by the intent, as in:

TP2 velocities.vec-v2d

Of course, this means that with TP2, you can't plot data from files that have a minus contained in the name, as this will be interpreted, truncating the file name.

Multiple Document Interface

Windows® recognizes what is called a *multiple document interface*, or MDI. TP2 is based around this concept, while Tecplot™ is not. Tecplot™ will only display a single context. TP2 will display up to 25 completely unrelated contexts, each in its own window. TP2 can be launched with wild cards:

TP2 *.v2d *.v3d *.2dv *.3dv

Animations

Tecplot™ will create animations—raster meta files (extension RM) for early versions and also audio visual interleave files (extension AVI) for recent versions. A utility, Framer, is provided with Tecplot™ to display the animations so created. AVI files can be displayed by various utilities. TP2 creates and also displays various animations in several formats, including GIF.

Examples

Tecplot™ comes with several excellent examples. These are separate files in a subfolder created during installation. TP2 comes with a variety of 2D and 3D examples, all of which are embedded inside the executable, so that you only need the EXE file with TP2. When you select a demo, TP2 creates the files and then displays the results. Both programs come with help files.

Data Processing

Both Tecplot™ and TP2 process data in a variety of ways, including interpolation, cutting, slicing, and translation from one form to another. TP2 has far more options for this because I added a feature every time I needed one for the work I was doing.

Drawings and Objects

TP2 will also read some AutoCAD™ files, including DXF and 3DS (3D Studio) as well as virtual reality markup language (VRML) files, which Tecplot™ will not import.

File Conversions

TP2 import many types of files, including several 3D formats. These may be written out to a different format, resulting in a file conversion. There are also many conversions available from the menu/convert.

Selecting Individual Elements

Individual elements may be selected by first setting *select 3D objects* from the options menu, then clicking on the desired elements. It will be useful to activate element borders, which can be done in the user options window, brought up from the menu/windows/user controls.

Appendix D. Hot Key Rotation

It is most convenient to control the view of 3D objects with the directional plus other control keys and to do so in steps. While many programs allow the user to select an item and then rotate it by dragging the mouse, this often results in ambiguous motions and irregular intervals. For example, angles in steps of 5° are usually adequate, as are displacements in steps of 5% of the display dimensions. This is easily accomplished in a Windows GUI by defining what are called *accelerators*. These are listed in the resource (.rc) file. A sample is listed below and a complete list can be found in keys.rc in the utilities folder.

```
FAST ACCELERATORS
  BEGIN
    "A",PUSH_ALT_A,VIRTKEY,ALT
    "B",PUSH_ALT_B,VIRTKEY,ALT
    "C",PUSH_ALT_C,VIRTKEY,ALT
    "A",PUSH_CTL_A,VIRTKEY,CONTROL
    "B",PUSH_CTL_B,VIRTKEY,CONTROL
    "C",PUSH_CTL_C,VIRTKEY,CONTROL
    "A",PUSH_CTL_ALT_A,VIRTKEY,CONTROL,ALT
    VK_F1,PUSH_F1,VIRTKEY
    VK_F4,PUSH_ALT_F4,VIRTKEY,ALT
    VK_LEFT,PUSH_SHIFT_LEFT,VIRTKEY,SHIFT
    VK_RIGHT,PUSH_SHIFT_RIGHT,VIRTKEY,SHIFT
  END
```

The commands are defined in another file (keys.h), a sample is listed below:

```
#define PUSH_ALT_A        0x0F00
#define PUSH_ALT_B        0x0F01
#define PUSH_ALT_C        0x0F03
#define PUSH_ALT_F4       0x0F0D
```

These must be loaded in WinMain() and placed inside the main message loop, as shown below:

```
int WINAPI WinMain(HINSTANCE hCurrent,HINSTANCE
    hPrevious,char*lCommand,int nShow)
  {
  HACCEL acc;
  acc=LoadAccelerators(hInst,"FAST");
  while(GetMessage(&msg,NULL,0,0))
    if(!TranslateAccelerator(msg.hwnd,acc,&msg))
      if(!TranslateMessage(&msg))
        DispatchMessage(&msg);
```

When the user presses one of these keys, a corresponding message is sent to the main procedure, where it can be processed, as illustrated below:

```
LRESULT WINAPI MainProc(HWND hWnd,DWORD wMsg,WPARAM
    wParam,LPARAM lParam)
  {
  if(wMsg==WM_COMMAND)
```

89

```
    {
    if(wParam==PUSH_UP)
      {
      Objective.a-=5;
      if(Objective.a<0)
        Objective.a=355;
      InvalidateRect(hPlot,NULL,FALSE);
      return(TRUE);
      }
    if(wParam==PUSH_DOWN)
      {
      Objective.a+=5;
      if(Objective.a>355)
        Objective.a=0;
      InvalidateRect(hPlot,NULL,FALSE);
      return(TRUE);
      }
    if(wParam==PUSH_LEFT)
      {
      Objective.c+=5;
      if(Objective.c>355)
        Objective.c=0;
      InvalidateRect(hPlot,NULL,FALSE);
      return(TRUE);
      }
    if(wParam==PUSH_RIGHT)
      {
      Objective.c-=5;
      if(Objective.c<0)
        Objective.c=355;
      InvalidateRect(hPlot,NULL,FALSE);
      return(TRUE);
      }
```

The call to `InvalidateRect()` forces the plot window to be repainted, which causes the scene to be rendered again by the OpenGL engine.

```
LRESULT WINAPI PlotProc(HWND hWnd,DWORD wMsg,WPARAM
  wParam,LPARAM lParam)
  {
  if(wMsg==WM_CLOSE)
    return(FALSE);
  if(wMsg==WM_CREATE)
    return(FALSE);
  if(wMsg==WM_DESTROY)
    return(FALSE);
  if(wMsg==WM_PAINT)
    {
    HDC hDC;
    PAINTSTRUCT ps;
```

```
hDC=BeginPaint(hWnd,&ps);
if(pDC)
    {
    if(hDC!=pDC)
        Abort(__LINE__,"OpenGL device context not
preserved");
    glRepaint(TRUE);
    }
EndPaint(hWnd,&ps);
return(FALSE);
}
if(wMsg==WM_SIZE)
    {
    PositionWindows();
    glRepaint(TRUE);
    return(FALSE);
    }
return(DefWindowProc(hWnd,wMsg,wParam,lParam));
}
```

In the GUI employed for these examples, the directional keys control scene rotations. Adding the alt key controls scene translation (i.e., pan). Adding the ctl key controls the light positioning. Pressing ctl-Z resets the scene, which was a useful combination implemented in early versions of AutoCAD.

Appendix E. Selection of Objects

In a Windows GUI, when the user clicks either button on the mouse, this send a message to the procedure assigned to that window. If it has no procedure (e.g., is a simple STATIC object), the message is sent to the procedure of the parent. There are four *click* messages:

```
WM_LBUTTONUP
WM_LBUTTONDOWN
WM_RBUTTONUP
WM_RBUTTONDOWN
```

These come with the mouse position combined in lParam, with the X position in the low part and Y position in the high part. These two parts are signed short (16-bit) integers. The location can be used with an inside polygon test to determine which object is being selected. There is also a

```
WM_MOUSEMOVE
```

message produced by dragging the mouse. You must save the initial position (i.e., DOWN message) and the final position (i.e., UP message) to create a rectangle followed by an inside polygon test. This presumes you know where the objects are displayed on the screen. If you have displayed the objects with Windows API calls or with some custom software, as discussed in the *other* section of the first book in this series, *3D Rendering in Windows with and without OpenGL*, then this may be the case. If, however, you are using the OpenGL rendering engine, you will not know where the objects end up on a pixel-by-pixel basic. For that, we use *stenciling*.

Appendix F. OpenGL Stenciling

The OpenGL rendering engine provides something called *stenciling*. While this feature has multiple uses, we will consider only one of those here. It's like a fourth dimension of color beyond red, green, and blue. Stencil bits are listed in the table in Appendix A. If you want to use stenciling, you must select a pixel context that provides this feature. While some systems may provide more than 8 stencil bits, I have never seen this on a Windows machine. This means that there can be no more than 256 distinct objects. Besides selecting the right context, there are a few commands that must come at the beginning of the rendering process:

```
glClearStencil(0);
glEnable(GL_STENCIL_TEST);
glStencilOp(GL_KEEP,GL_KEEP,GL_REPLACE);
glStencilFunc(GL_ALWAYS,0,-1);
```

The index (0-255) for each object is set before rendering with this call:

```
glStencilFunc(GL_ALWAYS,index,-1);
```

The index is retrieved by passing the XY location within the rendering window with this call:

```
glReadPixels(x,y,1,1,GL_STENCIL_INDEX,
   GL_UNSIGNED_INT,&index);
```

This code is implemented in several examples included in this series of three books, including View3D in *3D Articulation*; ETTP, knight, MSRE, museum, SandyRun, and SWSA5 in *3D Models in Motion*; and knight, stonehenge2, and View3DS in *3D Rendering*.

Stenciling is used here in the Knight's Tour example to identify the pieces and squares, for example, see "white king's rook" in the lower left hand corner.

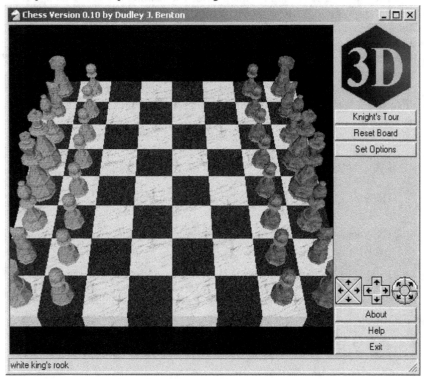

Figure 63. Use of Stenciling to Identify Objects in OpenGL

While OpenGL's stenciling works well enough to identify a few objects, it doesn't help when you need to select a few elements from among thousands. There is no limit to the number of 3D elements displayed or selected using TP2 but your only option is to save the modified model out to a new file and manipulate the results with some other software such as a text editor. Another option is presented in Appendix I.

Appendix G: Compilers

If you don't have a C compiler, I suggest either Digital Mars® or Microsoft®. The former can be downloaded free from the following link:

http://www.digitalmars.com/

The Microsoft® C compiler is also available free of charge. Simply download and install the W7.1 SDK and DDK. While these developer kits are no longer available at the Microsoft@ Download Center, they can be found elsewhere on the web. After you install the two kits, combine the bin, include, and lib folders and put them in a folder called something like C:\VC32 or C:\VC64. There will be several folders with similar names. If you are targeting a system with an Intel™ processor, the folders you need will have either x86 or x64 in them. There are four combinations of the two architectures. These arise from the O/S you are running them on and the O/S you are targeting. For instance, you can create a 64-bit executable on a 32-bit machine and vise versa. Unless you need more than 2GB of memory in a single program, 64-bit is not necessary, as 32-bit executables will run on either O/S. You will, however, need to create the specific target when creating Add-Ins for Excel, as these are not interchangeable.

The Intel™ C compiler touts extended features and convenient access to unlock the full power of their processors. I used it extensively at one time, but now see no advantage to it. The early Microsoft® C compilers were a dreadful mess of bugs and would croak if you turned on any of the optimization options. Sometime around 2005 Microsoft® fixed their C compiler, eliminating any need for the Intel™ C compiler.

Code Profiling

The Intel® compilers provide runtime profiling (i.e., function calls and timing), though somewhat cumbersome and expensive. In over 40 years I've never seen anything that comes close to Walter Bright's C compilers (originally Zortech™, then Symantec™, and now Digital Mars™). Simply add −gt and recompile to get a list of who called what, when, how many times, and how long each took. The convenience and simplicity is in a league of it's own—plus it's free! Walter Bright is a genius!

Appendix H. Rendering: How Long Does It Take?

Most of the examples accompanying this text render quite rapidly. The complex hair example takes several seconds, especially with the more complex options (e.g., style 1 or 2). There are some sections of code that might seem tedious (e.g., creating and smoothing polygons with the *hoop* hair style) so that you might wonder if these could be streamlined so as to decrease the rendering time. You might even think of saving the polygons and outward normals in arrays. After all, calculating the normals takes a cross product plus at least one hypotenuse. In one sweep through the normalization function is called over four million times. Wouldn't it be worth it to minimize this effort?

We can explore these questions with code profiling, as described at the bottom of Appendix G. You will find a batch file (_trace.bat) in the examples hair folder that will work with either the Synamtec™ or Digital Mars™ compilers to produce a *profiled* executable. The source code (hair.c) contains conditional compilation statements to implement the necessary differences, including disabling delayed painting and exiting after the first rendering. After the program finishes, there will be two files (trace.def and trace.log), which contain the profiling results. These are summarized in the table on the next page.

In this table we see 4,194,080 calls to Normalize(), which calls CrossProduct() so that it is also called 4,194,080 times. We see that the function taking the longest time for a single call is GetBestPixelFormat(), but it is only called once. Tree time is sum of the function plus everything that it calls so that the tree time for main program is the total runtime.

Consider the function times and the percentage column in particular. Tree time for RenderComplexTube() accounts for 84% of the total time. Tree time for Normalize() and CrossProduct() contribute only a little more than 4% each. The function itself (listed right after Equation 8.6) is not burdensome. The rendering engine calls:

```
glBegin(GL_QUAD_STRIP);
glNormal3d(p.x,p.y,p.z);
glVertex3f(w[i1].x,w[i1].y,w[i1].z);
glEnd();
```

are not profiled so we can't tell directly how long these take. We could, however, comment out the lines and run the program again. This exercise would be unnecessary because it is clear that most of the RenderComplexTube() time is spent inside the OpenGL rendering engine.

What does all this mean? The rendering part is by far the most time-consuming. Streamlining the code is somewhat pointless. Storing the polygons and normals in arrays is also pointless. After all that effort, you would hardly notice any difference in the time to render.

99

Table H1. Rendering Hair Once with Style Option 1

num calls	tree time μs	func time μs	func time %	per call μs	function name
24,648	30,010,214	27,216,402	84.14033%	1,104	RenderComplexTube
24,648	32,046,887	1,760,312	5.44206%	71	RenderHair
4,194,080	1,419,116	1,419,116	4.38724%	0	Normalize
4,194,080	1,377,402	1,377,402	4.25828%	0	CrossProduct
666,678	220,414	220,414	0.68142%	0	hypot3d
1	157,050	156,890	0.48503%	156,890	GetBestPixelFormat
1	32,166,691	102,810	0.31784%	102,810	RenderHead
148,731	46,636	46,636	0.14418%	0	xrand
1	11,714	11,714	0.03621%	11,714	ReadModel
4,314	11,484	9,994	0.03090%	2	glColor
24,648	7,732	7,732	0.02390%	0	drand
1	7,745	5,326	0.01647%	5,326	CreateWindows
394	2,801	2,433	0.00752%	6	AreaTriangle
6,286	1,943	1,943	0.00601%	0	sign
2	32,168,574	1,723	0.00533%	861	glRepaint
37	1,645	1,636	0.00506%	44	MainProc@16
4,321	1,492	1,492	0.00461%	0	floatColor
4	32,169,149	537	0.00166%	134	PositionWindows
1	32,346,458	521	0.00161%	521	main
6	426	423	0.00131%	70	CreatePushButton
3	292	292	0.00090%	97	Register
5	276	273	0.00084%	54	CreateRadioButton
72	474	160	0.00049%	2	QuickSortIndices
2	158	158	0.00049%	79	WindowText
16	32,169,149	48	0.00015%	3	PlotProc@16
16	39	38	0.00012%	2	LogoProc@16
1	302	9	0.00003%	9	RegisterClasses
1	6	6	0.00002%	6	GetResource
1	8	2	0.00001%	2	LoadBitmapResource
1	10	2	0.00001%	2	LoadBitmaps
9,292,999		32,346,442	100.00000%		

Appendix I. Splitting a Model Mathematically

It can be quite tedious to split a model into left, right, front, and back legs or other such categories by selecting one element at a time. Some models (VRML, for example, skeleton.wrl in the model folder of the online archive) may be already split into parts and have clear separators in the file:

```
geometry DEF LFEMUR010_FACES    IndexedFaceSet
geometry DEF LHAND010_FACES     IndexedFaceSet
geometry DEF LHUMERUS010_FACES  IndexedFaceSet
geometry DEF LKNEE010_FACES     IndexedFaceSet
geometry DEF MANDIBLE010_FACES  IndexedFaceSet
geometry DEF PELVIS010_FACES    IndexedFaceSet
```

while most others may not. Another option for splitting models is mathematically. This process involves tests such as less than or greater than and also inside polygon calculations. To illustrate this we will use the T-Rex model, which may be found in the examples\T-Rex folder. The complete model (zip file) is included in the online archive accompanying *3D Models in Motion*. It can be rendered with View3D, which may be found in the online archive accompanying the present text. It is shown in the figure below:

Figure 64. T-Rex Rendered by View3D

View3D will import the model from the zip file (as 3DS) and export it to 3DV format, which is far less convoluted and also not arcane binary. This format can be read in and written out using read3dv.c, which may be found in the utilities folder. We will process this model with split.c, which may be found in the examples\T-Rex folder. To assist in defining boundaries and polygons, we will also convert the model to an excel spreadsheet using 3dvtocsv.c, which may be found in the utilities folder. The result is in T-Rex.xls, shown below:

101

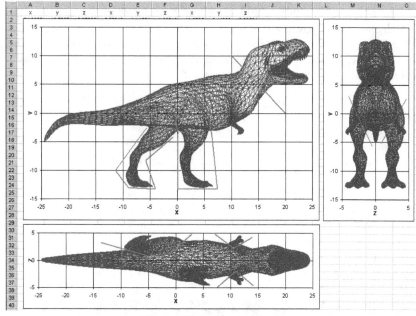

Figure 65. T-Rex in Excel

We read the model, process, and write it back out:

```
int main(int argc,char**argv,char**envp)
    {
    model=Read3DV("T-Rex.3dv");
    Split();
    Write3DV(&model,"split.3dv");
    return(0);
    }
```

We begin with the simplest test, that indicated by the downward-sloping diagonal line through the neck, y=20-x. If the centroid of an element (xc,yc,zc) is above this line, we change the color:

```
for(e=0;e<model.elems;e++)
    {
    i=model.elem[e].i;
    j=model.elem[e].j;
    k=model.elem[e].k;
    x1=model.node[i].x;
    y1=model.node[i].y;
    z1=model.node[i].z;
    x2=model.node[j].x;
    y2=model.node[j].y;
    z2=model.node[j].z;
    x3=model.node[k].x;
```

102

```
y3=model.node[k].y;
z3=model.node[k].z;
xc=(x1+x2+x3)/3.;
yc=(y1+y2+y3)/3.;
zc=(z1+z2+z3)/3.;
if(yc>20.-xc)
   model.elem[e].color=0xFF0000;
else
   model.elem[e].color=0x00FF00;
}
```

The result is:

Figure 66. Element Centroids with y>20-x

To select just the eyes, we apply the following test

```
r=hypot(xc-19.26,yc-11.26);
if(r<0.35&&fabs(zc)>1.18)
```

Figure 67. Element Centroids with r<0.35 and |zc|>1.18

The PolyEdit utility (available free at the same location as the online archive accompanying this text) is 2D but can be quite useful too.

Figure 68. PolyEdit Showing Right Leg Selection Polygon

A 3D inside polygon test would be rather useless, as a point satisfying the criteria would have to lie *exactly* in the plane formed by two perpendicular vectors, which is unlikely. A 2D inside polygon test is quite useful, especially when combined with a second criteria along the third axis. The code is listed below:

```
typedef struct{double x,y;}XY;
int InsidePolygon(XY*p,int n,double x,double y)
  {
  int above1,above2,i,right;
  double x1,x2,y1,y2;
  x2=p[n-1].x;
  y2=p[n-1].y;
  above2=y2>y?1:0;
  for(right=i=0;i<n;i++)
    {
    x1=x2;
    y1=y2;
    x2=p[i].x;
    y2=p[i].y;
    above1=above2;
    above2=y2>y?1:0;
    if(above1==above2)
      continue;
    if(x1>x&&x2>x)
      right++;
    else if(y1<y2)
      {
      if((x-x1)*(y2-y1)<(x2-x1)*(y-y1))
        right++;
      }
    else if(y1>y2)
      {
      if((x-x1)*(y2-y1)>(x2-x1)*(y-y1))
        right++;
      }
    }
  return(right&1);
  }
```

Note that the polygon is *not* closed. The polygon displayed in the preceding figure is:

```
XY poly[]={
  { 0.241,-10.490},
  { 0.948,-12.159},
  { 2.025,-13.213},
  { 3.563,-13.561},
  { 7.295,-13.152},
  { 6.671,-11.892},
  { 5.759,-11.205},
  { 4.265,-10.774},
  { 3.486, -9.338},
  { 3.691, -7.279},
```

```
{  5.288,  -5.670},
{  6.282,  -3.360},
{  6.210,  -1.174},
{  5.657,   0.292},
{  4.559,   1.265},
{  3.420,   1.828},
{  2.206,   2.012},
{  1.101,   1.495},
{  0.282,   0.540},
{ -0.189,  -1.473},
{ -0.036,  -2.971},
{  0.594,  -3.679},
{  0.903,  -5.217},
{  0.147,  -7.000},
{ -0.136,  -9.009}};
```

The test is:

```
if(InsidePolygon(poly,sizeof(poly)/sizeof(poly[0]),
    xc,yc)&&yc<-zc)
    model.elem[e].color=0xFF0000;
else
    model.elem[e].color=0x00FF00;
```

The result is:

Figure 69. Leg Polygon Selection

106

Appendix J. Texture-Linked Models

Some models (e.g., 3DS) consist of a set of elements plus one or more textures. The textures are often JPGs, but not always. There are many formats within the TIF specification so that reading any one of these would be quite tedious. It is more efficient to use PaintShop™ or PhotoShop™ to convert any TIFs to JPGs and repackage. I have found several models online that have the wrong name embedded in the 3DS file for the texture. I have been able to fix these with a binary editor, using a shorter file name or padding the tail with zeroes if necessary. One model referred to the same texture with two different names so that the same image was included twice—quite wasteful.

Not only are some of the texture references misspelled in 3DS files found on the web, there is often no file extension (e.g., JPG or TIF) so that this must be assumed or supplied externally. View3D tries BMP, GIF, and JPG. Also, 3DS does not necessarily conform to OpenGL standards, particularly in the area of textures. Therefore, some textures must be *adjusted* (i.e., resized) before the models can be rendered with OpenGL. This may also require changing the texture-to-vertex mapping. A resizing adjustment is always linear so that the coordinates can be easily modified (x'=a*x+b, y'=c*y+d). The coefficients (abcd) can be calculated with Excel. After that, read the model in (read3ds.c) and write it back out with the modified coordinates.

View3D expects the elements and textures to be contained within a single ZIP file and any textures to be stored in JPG format. You can repackage these if necessary so as to display them. View3D unzips the archive if necessary and places the files in the temporary folder. The location of the temporary folder in Windows can be seen in Control Panel/System/Advanced Settings/Environment Variables or by opening a command prompt and typing> set.

Programmatic access to ZIP files is provided by the code (ziplib.c) and header (ziplib.h), both located in the utilities folder of the online archive accompanying the current text. Extracting the files accomplished by:

```
void ExtractFiles(char*archive)
  {
  int i,n;
  size_t uncomp_size;
  void*bufr;
  mz_zip_archive zip;
  mz_zip_archive_file_stat stat;
  if(_access(archive,0))
    return;
  memset(&zip,0,sizeof(zip));
  if(mz_zip_reader_init_file(&zip,archive,0)==0)
    return;
  n=(int)mz_zip_reader_get_num_files(&zip);
  for(i=0;i<n;i++)
    {
```

107

```
    if(mz_zip_reader_is_file_a_directory(&zip,i))
      continue;
    if(!mz_zip_reader_file_stat(&zip,i,&stat))
      {
      mz_zip_reader_end(&zip);
      goto error;
      }

    if((bufr=mz_zip_reader_extract_file_to_heap(&zip,stat
    .m_filename,&uncomp_size,0))==NULL)
      goto error;
    if(uncomp_size!=stat.m_uncomp_size)
      goto error;
    this_file.comp_size=(size_t)stat.m_comp_size;

    if(FileCreate(stat.m_filename,bufr,(size_t)stat.m_unc
    omp_size,stat.m_time)<0)
      goto error;
    free(bufr);
    }
error:
  mz_zip_reader_end(&zip);
  }
```

Appendix K. Element Orientation

It is most often assumed that polygons are navigated in a counterclockwise direction. This presumption is as old as compass points:

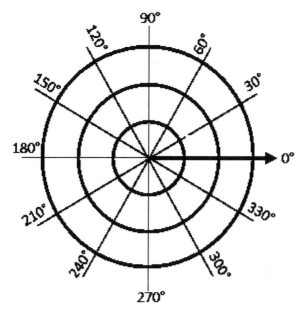

Figure 70. Counterclockwise Angles

Not all 3D models conform to this presumed orientation. You can select the orientation in OpenGL

```
glFrontFace(GL_CCW);
glFrontFace(GL_CW);
```

but this won't fix the specified outward normals, only the automatically calculated one.

```
glEnable(GL_AUTO_NORMAL);
glDisable(GL_AUTO_NORMAL);
```

If the model appears unreasonably dark, the elements are probably backwards (i.e., clockwise). You can read the model in and write it back out with the opposite vertex order using the code found in the utilities folder of the online archive.

109

also by D. James Benton

3D Models in Motion Using OpenGL, ISBN-9798652987701, Amazon, 2020 (book 2 in the 3D series.

3D Rendering in Windows: How to display three-dimensional objects in Windows with and without OpenGL, ISBN-9781520339610, Amazon, 2016 (book 1 in the 3D series).

A Synergy of Short Stories: The whole may be greater than the sum of the parts, ISBN-9781520340319, Amazon, 2016.

Azeotropes: Behavior and Application, ISBN-9798609748997, Amazon, 2020.

bat-Elohim: Book 3 in the Little Star Trilogy, ISBN-9781686148682, Amazon, 2019.

Boilers: Performance and Testing, ISBN: 9798789062517, Amazon 2021.

Combined 3D Rendering Series: 3D Rendering in Windows®, 3D Models in Motion, and 3D Articulation, ISBN-9798484417032, Amazon, 2021.

Complex Variables: Practical Applications, ISBN-9781794250437, Amazon, 2019.

Compression & Encryption: Algorithms & Software, ISBN-9781081008826, Amazon, 2019.

Computational Fluid Dynamics: an Overview of Methods, ISBN-9781672393775, Amazon, 2019.

Computer Simulation of Power Systems: Programming Strategies and Practical Examples, ISBN-9781696218184, Amazon, 2019.

Contaminant Transport: A Numerical Approach, ISBN-9798461733216, Amazon, 2021.

CPUnleashed! Tapping Processor Speed, ISBN-9798421420361, Amazon, 2022.

Curve-Fitting: The Science and Art of Approximation, ISBN-9781520339542, Amazon, 2016.

Death by Tie: It was the best of ties. It was the worst of ties. It's what got him killed., ISBN-9798398745931, Amazon, 2023.

Differential Equations: Numerical Methods for Solving, ISBN-9781983004162, Amazon, 2018.

Equations of State: A Graphical Comparison, ISBN-9798843139520, Amazon, 2022.

Evaporative Cooling: The Science of Beating the Heat, ISBN-9781520913346, Amazon, 2017.

Forecasting: Extrapolation and Projection, ISBN-9798394019494, Amazon 2023.

Heat Engines: Thermodynamics, Cycles, & Performance Curves, ISBN-9798486886836, Amazon, 2021.

Heat Exchangers: Performance Prediction & Evaluation, ISBN-9781973589327, Amazon, 2017.

Heat Recovery Steam Generators: Thermal Design and Testing, ISBN-9781691029365, Amazon, 2019.

Heat Transfer: Heat Exchangers, Heat Recovery Steam Generators, & Cooling Towers, ISBN-9798487417831, Amazon, 2021.

Heat Transfer Examples: Practical Problems Solved, ISBN-9798390610763, Amazon, 2023.

The Kick-Start Murders: Visualize revenge, ISBN-9798759083375, Amazon, 2021.

Jamie2: Innocence is easily lost and cannot be restored, ISBN-9781520339375, Amazon, 2016-18.

Kyle Cooper Mysteries: Kick Start, Monte Carlo, and Waterfront Murders, ISBN-9798829365943, Amazon, 2022.

The Last Seraph: Sequel to Little Star, ISBN-9781726802253, Amazon, 2018.

Little Star: God doesn't do things the way we expect Him to. He's better than that! ISBN-9781520338903, Amazon, 2015-17.

Living Math: Seeing mathematics in every day life (and appreciating it more too), ISBN-9781520336992, Amazon, 2016.

Lost Cause: If only history could be changed..., ISBN-9781521173770, Amazon, 2017.

Mass Transfer: Diffusion & Convection, ISBN-9798702403106, Amazon, 2021.

Mill Town Destiny: The Hand of Providence brought them together to rescue the mill, the town, and each other, ISBN-9781520864679, Amazon, 2017.

Monte Carlo Murders: Who Killed Who and Why, ISBN-9798829341848, Amazon, 2022.

Monte Carlo Simulation: The Art of Random Process Characterization, ISBN-9781980577874, Amazon, 2018.

Nonlinear Equations: Numerical Methods for Solving, ISBN-9781717767318, Amazon, 2018.

Numerical Calculus: Differentiation and Integration, ISBN-9781980680901, Amazon, 2018.

Numerical Methods: Nonlinear Equations, Numerical Calculus, & Differential Equations, ISBN-9798486246845, Amazon, 2021.

Orthogonal Functions: The Many Uses of, ISBN-9781719876162, Amazon, 2018.

Overwhelming Evidence: A Pilgrimage, ISBN-9798515642211, Amazon, 2021.

Particle Tracking: Computational Strategies and Diverse Examples, ISBN-9781692512651, Amazon, 2019.

Plumes: Delineation & Transport, ISBN-9781702292771, Amazon, 2019.

Power Plant Performance Curves: for Testing and Dispatch, ISBN-9798640192698, Amazon, 2020.

Practical Linear Algebra: Principles & Software, ISBN-9798860910584, Amazon, 2023.

Props, Fans, & Pumps: Design & Performance, ISBN-9798645391195, Amazon, 2020.

Remediation: Contaminant Transport, Particle Tracking, & Plumes, ISBN-9798485651190, Amazon, 2021.

ROFL: Rolling on the Floor Laughing, ISBN-9781973300007, Amazon, 2017.

Seminole Rain: You don't choose destiny. It chooses you, ISBN-9798668502196, Amazon, 2020.

Septillionth: 1 in 10^{24}, ISBN-9798410762472, Amazon, 2022.

Software Development: Targeted Applications, ISBN-9798850653989, Amazon, 2023.

Software Recipes: Proven Tools, ISBN-9798815229556, Amazon, 2022.

Steam 2020: to 150 GPa and 6000 K, ISBN-9798634643830, Amazon, 2020.

Thermochemical Reactions: Numerical Solutions, ISBN-9781073417872, Amazon, 2019.

Thermodynamic and Transport Properties of Fluids, ISBN-9781092120845, Amazon, 2019.

Thermodynamic Cycles: Effective Modeling Strategies for Software Development, ISBN-9781070934372, Amazon, 2019.

Thermodynamics - Theory & Practice: The science of energy and power, ISBN-9781520339795, Amazon, 2016.

Version-Independent Programming: Code Development Guidelines for the Windows® Operating System, ISBN-9781520339146, Amazon, 2016.

The Waterfront Murders: As you sow, so shall you reap, ISBN-9798611314500, Amazon, 2020.

Weather Data: Where To Get It and How To Process It, ISBN-9798868037894, Amazon, 2023.

About the Author: D. James Benton is married to his high school sweetheart, has three wonderful daughters and six grandchildren. He lives in Tennessee on a little farm next to a creek. He is now retired after working in the power industry for forty years with a PhD in Mechanical Engineering. His specialties include: thermodynamics, heat transfer, and software development. His life was turned around at seventeen while visiting a mission hospital in Kenya, The Lighthouse for Christ.

This is a third course on three-dimensional rendering of models, building on my previous books, 3D Rendering in Windows and 3D Models in Motion. In this text we will cover spatial manipulation of objects in order to create the appearance of specific articulation. We also cover finer details, including hair or fur. The Windows® operating system and OpenGL® rendering engine will be our platform, but the same principles apply equally well to other environments. We assume the reader is familiar with C and programming for the Windows® operating system and will not dwell on those details. Many references are available on these foundational subjects, including my book, Version Independent Programming. As in that text, we require that all code function properly on any version and configuration of Windows®. All of the software and associated files described herein is available free online.

ISBN 9798596362480